BUILT TO LAST

DESIGNING & MAINTAINING A PASSIONATE, LOVING AND LASTING RELATIONSHIP

GEOFF LAUGHTON

Built to Last: Designing & Maintaining a Passionate, Loving, and Lasting Relationship

by Geoff Laughton

Cover Design by Melodye Hunter
Typesetting: Zonoiko Arafat
Cover Design by Melodye Hunter
Copyright © 2015 by Geoff Laughton

ISBN: 978-0-9964269-4-7

Crescendo Publishing, LLC
300 Carlsbad Village Drive
Ste. 108A, #443
Carlsbad, California 92008-2999

www.CrescendoPublishing.com
GetPublished@CrescendoPublishing.com

A Message from the Author

Click on the video of the link to hear a personal message from Geoff Laughton, author of Built To Last

https://vimeo.com/133511004

To further support you through your journey, remember to download your complimentary bonus gifts at http://www.builttolastbook.com/

What People Are Saying About "Built to Last"

"For men and women grappling with understanding each other in love relationships, this book is a "must!" It moves couples in the direction of improving intimacy and making better connections with straight-forward language, road-tested perspectives, tools, and a deep understanding of both genders' needs and approaches."

Marni Battista,

Founder of "Dating with Dignity," Coach, and Frequent TV commentator on dating & relationship; www.datingwithdignity.com

"Geoff Laughton has written a grounded, intelligent, guide to having a real relationship, one that grows and lasts. This book feels like sitting down with a kind and sane guide, and one who has walked his talk. Geoff's love and the book's practicality are refreshing, comforting, and confidence- building."

Tama Kieves,

USA Today-featured visionary career coach and New York Times best-selling author of "Inspired & Unstoppable: Wildly Succeeding in Your Life's Work!" and "This Time, I Dance: Creating the Work You Love" www.tamakieves.com

"This book is a guide that any couple can use to be able to proactively approach starting a conscious relationship from the very beginning, sacredly build that relationship, and then have great tools to lovingly maintain it for years to come."

Rachael Jayne Groover,

Author of "Powerful and Feminine" and Creator of Art of Feminine Presence™

"After all that we do to help people find love, it's great to see a new book on the scene that helps set couples up for success from the very start, and supports them through what is hopefully a long journey together. Geoff's metaphor of relationship being like designing, building, and maintaining a house really works to make the material easy to understand and put to use immediately."

Orna and Matthew Walters,

Renowned Dating & Relationship Coaches at CreatingLoveOnPurpose.com

Geoff's expertise and heart speak especially strongly to us men, who must navigate the treacherous seas of emotional awareness and vulnerability that are so necessary to forge lasting relationships! The world needs this book!

Rick Broniec, MEd.,

Author of "The Seven Generations Story: An Incentive to Heal Yourself, Your Family and the Planet" and "A Passionate Life: Seven Steps for Reclaiming Your Passion, Purpose and Joy."

"Straight talk from the heart...this book not only supplies it, but teaches us how to do it. Built To Last gives us access to powerful and free relationships by showing us how to communicate our needs and joys with deep truth and compassion for ourselves and others."

Dr. Martin Kettelhut, Ph.D.,

Author of "Listen...Until You Disappear"

"Geoff has plenty of lived experience that has helped him gift us with a solid, useful book. Taking us from how we first find love, he guides us step-by-step, into the essential qualities of a healthy, long-term relationship and how to actually build it and keep it vibrantly alive. I suggest reading it out loud together with your partner."

Bill Kauth,

Co-founder of the New Warrior Training Adventure of the Mankind Project and author of "A Circle of Men" and "We Need Each Other: Building Gift Community"

"I've read a lot of books out telling women how to nurture relationships, but not many offer guidance to men in a way they can get it intellectually and emotionally. This book finally fills that void with humorous, informative, down-to-earth, practical wisdom that speaks to men's hearts AND minds without excluding benefits to women."

Frantonia Pollins

Author of "The Sexy Side of Success: Redefining Feminine Leadership, from the Boardroom to the Bedroom"
www.FrantoniaPollins.com

Dedication

This book is dedicated – with enormous gratitude – to the most important forces and gifts in my life:

My family, Sarah, Marc, and Tom, all of whom have taught me the most valuable ways of loving – and being loved - unconditionally;

My late mother, Vickie Carder, who helped hone me into the healer I've become; my Dad, Gerald R. Carder, who taught me more than I have room to tell about here (or could be printed in a book that youngsters might get their hands on); my late maternal grandmother, Caroline Eberman Laughton, without whom I probably would not have survived to adolescence or stayed out of prison; my late Uncle, William M. Laughton, who showed me love and mentorship when I didn't have a male role model yet available to me; my Beloved Sister Caroline, who I treasure every day as a best friend and gift from Spirit;

The late Don Lehmkuhl, who opened the curtain for me, at 15, to the gifts and talents I wouldn't remember to use for another 20 years; Dean Spillane Walker, who began showing me the path to my true self 52 years ago and is still a great teacher for me; Katy, Barbara, and Sheri, who taught a teenager and young man about what he had to offer as a lover & partner that got me beautifully prepared for the Love of My Life, Sarah; David Rubine, who taught me one of the most important life lessons ever on top of a cliff in Hollister, CA and remains a brother and one of my dearest (and true) friends; and Jill

Hesseltine Medina, who's love and gratitude has gotten me back on track more times than she could know;

My Spiritual Teacher, Phaeryn Sheehan, who pulled me out of so much darkness into *so* much Light; my Sisters from Spirit, Shakti Dudley and Joyea Pascoe, who've mentored, taught, and saved me more times than you could possibly ever know; and Denny Gregg, who began the path towards healing an inner child named Geoff and awakened a whole different career I wouldn't have anticipated in a million years;

Marty Kettelhut, who is the younger brother I never had and always wanted; Drew Semel, who led me into the men's work that spawned this book and all my passion with men's work; Julie Michaels Knell, who's never stopped nudging me (with infinite patience) towards letting the writer in me actually get out.

My business and life coach, Ronda Wada, who was the first coach to *really* get me & my Soul's mission and has relentlessly *and* lovingly reminded me of that mission every time I've struggled with claiming it;

And, lastly, Spirit...in all the forms and ways It comes to me, guides me, awakens me, and sources me in ways that I could never adequately express my gratitude for.

All of these precious beings, guides, and forces of the Divine have truly inspired and molded me into the kind of man, so far, I could only once dream of being.

Table of Contents

Section III

Maintaining Your Built-to-Last Relationship

Section IV

From Happily Ever After to Bliss

Introduction

The Building Blocks of a Relationship Built to Last

About twenty years ago, a dear, respected teacher of mine encouraged me to remember that, "Women are powerful people pretending to be hopeless romantics, and Men are hopeless romantics pretending to be powerful people."

All these years later, that statement sticks in my head (and heart). I've come to see how, for both myself and the scores of men I've worked with (not to mention hundreds of women), that's *absolutely* the case. Yet, there's a fundamental disconnect happening with too many men and our ability to really know how to think, feel, and operate from the neck down a lot of the time. That's a big part of why this book is primarily a book for men of all orientations (though I trust that many women involved with men – or wanting to be – will appreciate and make good use of what's here). Men have *such* deep hearts, yet by and large, many of us were never taught how to navigate life and relationships from there. Instead, we've been reinforced in defaulting to our "hardwiring" to provide, produce, and protect ... and, if there's any room left for anything else, then focus on getting laid, and then see what's up with your heart later. Oh, and the other big piece of conditioning: whatever else you do, be sure that you try to figure it all out yourself. This has turned out to be a huge setup for men (and women) to fail and here's why.

The divorce rate seems to be holding steady at a too-high level near 50% for first-time marriages (and higher for subsequent ones), but marriage rates have been dropping significantly. While men are certainly not entirely to blame for the high levels of divorce, it's certainly revealing that, in twenty years of being a relationship coach, I can count on half a hand how many men have initiated contact with me to get help with their relationship. It's also disheartening to be aware of how many women are so frustrated in how to effectively understand and work with the Male Ego and all the habits that go with it.

I'll give you a few other statistics that are examples of why we need to stop setting ourselves and our children up to fail in relationships. In a recent study done by Dan Bilsker and Jennifer White in the *British Columbia Medical Journal*, suicide rates among men are three to four times higher than among women ... and marital breakdown seems to be a factor in many such situations with men. North American men going through divorce are eight times more likely than divorcing women to commit suicide, according to a research study done at the University of California, Riverside. For this study, Professor Augustine Kposowa wrote, "The reasons divorced men—as well as men in other situations—commit suicide much more often relate to shame, loss of identity, loneliness, separation from children, financial pressures, job troubles, cultural stereotypes and lack of social support." In addition, according to a report issued by the Samaritan organization that examined twenty-seven different studies of suicide, "The majority of studies suggest that men are at a greater risk of suicide than women in the aftermath of a relationship breakdown."

Now, I'm not sharing this because I want to be a buzzkill. I'm sharing it because it supports one thing that I've seen for years and years, which is the Lone Ranger paradigm of being a man—in and/or out of relationship—really doesn't work and at too high a cost. It contributes to killing men and leaving children fatherless. As a husband who's been blessed with 33 years and counting of a marriage I treasure, and as a father, this is unacceptable...and unnecessary.

This is why this book exists. A new paradigm needs to be built for how men—and the men or women who love and "hate" them—can engage in conscious, playful, vibrant, and fulfilling relationships. We also have to start debunking that myth that men are or should be the "strong, silent type" simply because we're men. We get that way because we've been culturally and unconsciously trained to be that way. Fortunately, that training can be shifted when desired.

In *my* experience, women want men who—yes—are strong. But women often define "strong" very differently from the way men do. I haven't found that women want their guys to be women, but they want them to be present and vulnerable when they dare. [Note: this book is not limited to heterosexual relationships, but – for ease of dealing with pronouns in particular, I'll be generally referring to how heterosexual men and women seem to operate. For LGBT readers, I invite you to make the substitutions from your experiences that fit for you.]

You know, boys learn to build with Legos, teenage boys can learn how to build stuff in high school shop classes, and—if we're lucky—in college, men are encouraged to begin figuring out what kind of life they want to build when they have minimal skills for doing so at that age. As adults, we then feel the drive to build a good life, a good family maybe, and a good living. Once that's done, then we can supposedly relax and enjoy the fruits of our labors by the time we're in our fifties, sixties, and beyond.

Yet rarely in that trajectory are we taught how to actually build a lasting, inspiring, sacred, passionate, and conscious love relationship. In my practice, I've seen that women don't tend to fare any better in terms of being trained how to co-create a conscious relationship. Teenage boys are mostly left to learn how to build a relationship from their peers (who usually suck at it just as badly), and girls are left to *their* peers, magazines, and the media ... many of which stay on the surface, really, and are still heavily weighted to a male viewpoint.

So, what's an earnest male and an equally earnest, loving partner to do? Well, this book aims to be a good start to teaching what's actually possible. From the 33 years of being in a perfectly imperfect marriage, where we've held on to loving and liking each other more often than not—combined with 20 years of experience coaching a very large number of people in how to have the relationship with themselves and a partner that really fills the bill for them—I've learned that one really useful pathway is to approach creating a conscious relationship much like you'd design, build, and maintain your dream home.

That's what this book is going to offer you: three essential building blocks needed to create your ideal relationship ... your dream relationship. Unlike a lot of how-to books on relationships, this book will not promise you Happily Ever After if you use what I'm going to share here. In fact, if that's what you're hoping for, best to look elsewhere, because you deserve a relationship that's strong, durable, beautiful, superbly constructed, and built to last (imagine that!). If you go for that, over Happily Ever After, you have a much stronger likelihood of having a life and a relationship that lasts for decades and consistently grows all along the way.

The structure of the book is in the same sequence that goes into building a Dream Home: designing it, building it, and maintaining it well. Section I – the Design Section – covers many of the elements I've seen that it takes to design or (re)design a conscious relationship that fits the Built To Last framework, including a description of some of the key structural flaws that plague many relationships (there are many). Any that you recognize you've done (or not) don't necessarily mean there's something wrong with you (or your partner); rather, they more reflect the lack of training in how to be a conscious man in the first place, much less a conscious partner and father. It all starts with having the best possible design for a relationship, which always starts with designing a foundation that's going to hold up that relationship for decades – and challenges - to come. That section details some key things to watch out for and how to best design that foundation in a realistic, but advanced way.

Once you've got a pretty great design done, for both the foundation and the house itself, the next step is to build it all—exterior and interior construction are equally important. This is where Section II comes in ... Laying The Foundation & Building The House To Last. This part of the book will show you the key things you want to do to lay the foundation you'll have already worked hard to design and then actually *build* a built-to-last relationship, including - in vivid detail - where cracks and breakdowns can be most likely to happen and how to either avoid them altogether or mitigate them, if you've already fallen into any of these kinds of problems/issues. For example, you'll learn how many people you really have in bed with you besides the two of you, how to radically improve communication, and what intimacy is and what it isn't, just to name a few things.

Once you've built the house/relationship, a key element to ensuring it lasts for years and years—with joy and fulfillment more often than not—is to have a plan for ongoing preventive maintenance, as opposed to just fixing leaks or cracks as they come up. I'm all about proactivity over reactivity. So Section III will cover Maintaining the New Foundation. Here you'll learn things like how to establish the right priorities in an ongoing manner; when it might be time to actually end a relationship (if the maintenance has been ignored for too long); and how to keep forwarding the action in ways that help you have a blissful relationship (which, as you'll see, does *not* mean perpetual happiness), rather than shooting for a bullshit-ridden Jerry Maguire paradigm of Happily Ever After.

There are thousands of relationship books out there. You will read ideas and perspectives in here that may not be brand new to you. This isn't meant to be the comprehensive Bible of Relationship. What it *is* meant to be is a tool for helping men (and, again, the women and men striving to understand the beast) wake up to what's really possible if they're willing to learn, let go of attachments to their historical stories about themselves (and the gender itself), and risk being vulnerable. It's meant to be practical and impractical, in the sense that real transformation doesn't tend to jive well with practicality all the time. More than anything, I wanted to share experiences and perspectives that are presented less from an academic viewpoint but more from over three decades of experience being in the trenches with this stuff, as a husband and father myself, in addition to having helped and guided over 1,000 people through the challenges and minefields.

So, I invite you to be willing to read this book with a *very* open mind and equally open heart. I hope you'll read it with a commitment to allowing yourself—during the reading and practicing of any of what's in the book—to immerse yourself in the V word. No, I'm not referring to *that* V word. I'm talking about *vulnerability* ... that quality that a lot of boys and men are pressured to hold as a four-letter word ... or an unambiguous sign of weakness. As Dr. Brene Brown has explained in great depth in her books *The Gifts of Imperfection* and *Daring Greatly*, there can be no wholehearted happiness or fulfillment without daring to be vulnerable. To my fellow men, I contend that vulnerability and presence are two of the most mandatory elements needed to have the kind of relationship that isn't just possible, but is the one you each deserve. If you don't master those two qualities and skills, you'll find it very challenging to have a self-respecting and self-actualizing partner hang around.

There's no more important journey to be taking in these times. My commitment to everyone reading this book is that the level of consciousness, skill, mastery, and – most importantly – love that can come from the perspective and approach laid out in this book will change your world. One of the strongest hopes we have for changing the world at-large – particularly for your children, grandchildren, and all future descendants – is you making conscious loving and relationship (of all kinds) your top priority and your most precious achievement. Let's get to it!

Section I

Designing a Relationship to Avoid Structural Flaws

Up until a few years ago, the idea of "relationship design" hadn't really occurred to me, in spite of the fact that I'd been doing it with couples for near onto two decades. When I decided to write this book, and began looking newly at my approach to relationship work through the figurative eyes of the architectural metaphor, I had one of those V8 moments. It was a moment where I realized that, over and over again, one of the most consistent predictors of serious relationship flaws—if not failure—has so much to do with what happens (and more to the point, what *doesn't* happen) at the beginning of a lot of "serious relationships." SO much heartache and heartbreak could have such a better chance of being lessened, if not prevented, by having a much more conscious way of kicking things off inside of a designing kind of framework. [This is also true, by the way, of couples who have been together a long long time who are finding things stale to putrid, or just plain mundane and mediocre ... it's rarely too late to re-design a relationship. In fact, I highly recommend it as a periodic commitment to practice.] This Section introduces some of the key elements that I believe need to be considered and explored with great heart and mindfulness during and after that lovely hormonally infused merging period we all experience in the early stages of a relationship ... otherwise known as the endorphin-saturated obsession/infatuation period where everything *seems* near perfect and you're reminded of just how horny two people could actually get with each other on a daily basis. Not to be a buzz-kill, but that period wears off; hence, it's VERY helpful to bring in conscious design considerations and elements in between rounds of good old-fashioned Doing the Do.

Consequently, you'll be reading about such things as the relationship between compatibility and lust, how to build a really strong foundation, the dangers of expectations and role-playing (both inside and outside the bedroom), where you can use Spirituality in a proactive way to design a long-lasting relationship, and how to not let sex cloud your design judgment (while still enjoying it, mind you).

Let's get right to the drawing board!

Chapter 1

Love, Lust, & Compatibility

Love, Lust, & Compatibility

Two of my favorite things in life are love and lust. They've been very important elements in the evolution of my own marriage. However, you do not want to base your decision that you and your potential (or actual) partner are meant to be partners for life on them. You do *not* want your crotch picking your partners; it's not even remotely reliable biologically, emotionally, mentally, or Spiritually.

One variable that gets short shrift, and is a *much* more reliable factor in picking the right relationship and partner, is *compatibility*. But you have to realize that compatibility does not get automatically conferred through hormonal attraction. In fact, the vast majority of couples who've come to work with me complain that their relationship doesn't feel like it used to. They wonder why lust fades and if that means that *the love* has faded.

According to several psychological and biological studies, there's no doubt about the certainty that infatuation and lust – as most people experience them in the beginnings of an intense attraction and love - will inevitably fade. Psychologist Dorothy Tennov's study that measured the duration of romantic love, from the moment infatuation hit to when a "feeling of neutrality" for one's love object began, was published in *Psychology Today*. What her study found was that the most frequent interval, as well as the average, was between eighteen months and three years. A different study hypothesized that the brain "cannot eternally maintain the revved up site of romantic bliss. If you want a situation where you and your long-term partner can still get very excited about each other, you will have to work on it, because in some ways you are bucking a biological tide." This is why it's important to know the definitions of—and the differences between—love, lust, and compatibility. Without this understanding, you just get yourself into all kinds of trouble.

Lust is largely biological attraction. There's one theory being investigated that we all have what sexologist John Money calls "Love Maps." These are "mental maps, or a template, replete with brain circuitry that determines what arouses you sexually, what drives you to fall in love with one person rather than another." While I believe that lust, combined with love, is an incredible thing, on a biological level, they're not the same thing. They're just great dancing partners. Romantics that hope for love at first sight may find what they think that is, but it's far more likely to be lust at first sight. In and of itself, that's not a problem—unless you're confusing lust for love and compatibility. If that's what you're doing, you don't know what you could be in for.

Love involves several tangibles and intangibles. In spite of years of research on love—what it is, why it is, etc.—when I look at the most successful relationships I've seen (and have been in myself), there always seem to be that "mystery" to them. When I met my wife, Sarah, neither of us was looking for a relationship. We came from vastly different backgrounds, different kinds of family history, different likes and dislikes, etc. No one looking from the outside, including our parents, could have ever imagined us being a great match, especially for thirty-three years (so far!). What bridges the gap between the impermanency of lust and hormonally activated attraction or infatuation and an enduring relationship? Well, love is certainly a big part of it.

I'm not going to try to define love here, but I sure know it when I *feel* it. One thing that distinguishes love from lust is that love is more emotionally centered. Lust is much more physically centered and tends to be felt the most in a few specific areas of our bodies (ahem). Because we know that lust can fade, we can also surmise that keeping love vital and long-lasting requires much more of us—and our faculties—than simply being turned on and horny. So, love can be seen as a multifaceted thing that requires much more than lust alone. One thing that helps organize and cohere a deeper, emotional love is having enough compatibility between the two of you to help sustain the relationship in challenging times ... growth times ... that are inevitable.

Compatibility does not mean that you and your partner would/should/could have identical likes, dislikes, morals, preferences, and values. It does mean, however, that you're in sync enough to be able to combine those kinds of qualities and orientations in such a way that you're able to co-create a wonderful, true synergy. The couples I've worked with that ultimately didn't make it are almost always people who either weren't really compatible in the first place and/or didn't really know that compatibility is not the kind of thing you get from the Geek Squad, install, and then just run on for the rest of your life. We all change over time (hopefully) and so will some of the factors that impact compatibility. It's not a given that that's "fatal." It's just a given that you want to be paying attention to those changes ongoingly over time.

Let me give you an example of what I'm talking about. When Sarah and I first met, she came from a fundamentalist Christian background, and I was—at the time—steadfastly against being with anyone who even uttered the word "God" much less anything fundamentalist. She was more the prim and proper type of person, and I was a very liberal, northern California–raised radical who'd had sex in my parents' home when they were there (with their permission, I might add), and who veered far to the left of anything religious, conservative, or straight and narrow. When we met, I was just a year out of school, in my first corporate job, making a whopping $11 an hour. Sarah had recently been divorced (for the second time from the same husband), had an eight-year-old son, had experienced having to raise that son by herself with minimal support from her ex, and had had to make the hard decision to leave the church she'd been raised in from birth when she realized that there were fundamental differences between what she knew to be best for her and what the church would endorse.

The hardest thing *I'd* ever had to deal with, up to that point, was figuring out where I could score the best pot, how I could live on $11 an hour, and how I was going to really trust any woman again after having my heart absolutely shattered by my last relationship, which had ended three years before I met Sarah. On the surface, you couldn't imagine (or at least I couldn't) two more disparate, incompatible people. Yet when fate threw us together on a chilly northern California night, where we had a two- to three-hour conversation, I discovered that compatibility had way more to do with deeper things than what we liked or not, what kind of language we might use (I had a potty mouth, even back then, while she talked like a good church girl), what our political leanings were, etc. In fact, for the first few weeks we dated (and didn't have sex), I wasn't feeling a lot of lust for her. My heart was definitely hooked. I thought she was gorgeous, yet I wasn't walking around with constant wild sexual fantasies about her, waiting to be unleashed. What I *was* clear on, right off the bat, was that I *liked* her. I *respected* her.

We both discovered that we prized respect and feeling safe with someone over how much we may have seemed to have in common, or how badly either of us wanted to get into each other's pants (though once that happened, we definitely had that eighteen months to three years of loving like rabbits). Over the life of our relationship, the things that mattered most to us in 1982—the things that helped establish a strong, mutual sense that we were compatible with each other—have shifted many times. But, because we had two of the mandatory things I think you have to have to be truly compatible with someone— liking each other and respecting each other—we've been able to each grow, change our likes and dislikes, evolve our personal and joint desires, and *remain* very compatible. We didn't confuse sexual desire for liking each other. We were both smart enough to know that we had to spend a significant amount of time gauging whether there were *enough* common interests, shared values, and dreams for our future to really get a sense of each other's character and heart.

Those are two other qualities that must be present for compatibility to be in place: knowing each other's true character (demonstrated consistently over more time than most people seem to spend "courting" these days) and the true nature of one's heart, which can help you get through any number of life's challenges that tend to fell a lot of the relationships I've encountered over the years.

To maintain long-term compatibility, there's no way to avoid the fact that you really do have to work (and play) at it. I've come to see that you can't have a successful relationship without love, but love is not enough on its own to ensure a lifetime of vibrant, passionate, and enduring connection with your partner. Sarah and I still have that, but we've changed in so many ways over all these years (for example, Sarah's now able to match me in the potty mouth department). You have to know what really matters the most to each of you. You have to know that SO well that, when you're in a major disagreement with each other, you can use those most non-negotiable priorities to help you decide what battles are worth fighting and which aren't.

You also know you've got some strong compatibility when neither of you allows a fight or disagreement to separate you (for more than a day or three). You learn to use your differences and diversity to keep your ongoing relationship interesting. I, for example, have always been a rabid music fan. Sarah didn't really care much about music when we first started dating. However, out of her love for me—and the attendant desire to learn more about what mattered to me—she's come to like a LOT of the music I love (though I haven't converted her over to AC/DC yet). I have come to really appreciate her mastery with color, design, décor, and making any environment physically and energetically gorgeous. Now we have both of those arenas to talk about, explore, and learn about together.

In other words, compatibility has less to do with how much you have in common in certain areas and much more to do with mutual flexibility, curiosity, exploratory bents, and how well you continually evolve your way of communicating with each other evermore deeply and currently. Once you both realize that the true fire in your relationship comes more authentically *after* the initial *heat* wears off, you both have so much more potential to keep your relationship growing until one of you takes your last breath.

It's important to note here that you *cannot* will compatibility into being. If it ain't there, it ain't there. I worked with a man who had been married for several years and knew, pretty early on, that his girlfriend-then-wife was very sweet and paid lots of loving attention to him that felt wonderful (since he had been raised with very little attention and care shown to him by his parents). However, all the kinds of activities that he liked to do were of no interest to her—none. Additionally, it became clear that there was little-to-no sexual chemistry between them. They ended up getting married, stayed together for several years essentially as roommates, and ultimately got divorced when they realized they couldn't force something into being that was counter to who they each really were.

A few final things I've seen help establish and maintain organically evolving compatibility—elements you want to look for in first year or two of your relationship (notice I said "year or two," not the first three to six months you've known each other? That's likely letting your crotch do the thinking)—include a shared love of porn ... *intellectual* porn. You *do* have to have *some* areas of mutually compatible intellectual capacity and interests. When the loins are being quiet for a spell (which can happen with age and children), you can get off in a very satisfying way when you can generate interesting and stimulating conversation with each other and with friends. Also, another key thing to know and remember is that the highest and best compatibility has to involve your mind, body, heart, and Spirit. The more those four domains get used and cultivated with each other and separately, the less you'll be without some edge of growth and evolution that will keep your relationship interesting and fun.

My experience has been that this tends to come more naturally for women. Men get caught up in wanting things to be the same; if things are "good" or "fine" now, why mess with changing anything? That will be the death of your energetic relationship, eventually (longevity is not a useful gauge of marital success and harmony; for a long time, it's been more predominantly a gauge of people's capacity for suffering, toleration, and resignation). So, in the "early days" of creating an unassailable foundation for your relationship, be sure you have *several* conversations about how each of you relate to change. If you're on two totally different planets about change, you're probably not going to be a very compatible fit over the long haul.

Lastly, I want to mention an especially important factor that's a part of compatibility: values. I'm blown away by how many couples don't talk in the early days about what their values are, particularly in the areas of children, parenting, money, health, master life values, and sex. I suspect that a big reason for this is that younger people don't tend to be that focused on them until they *have* to be (my judgment, anyway), and people can unconsciously confuse patterns of behavior as synonymous with values ... which just isn't a good idea. See the next chapter for more on this.

Chapter 2

A Strong Foundation Requires Knowing What You Really Want, Why, and For What Purpose

A Strong Foundation Requires Knowing What You Really Want, Why, and For What Purpose

Here's a very common sequence for how the average American relationship gets started: First, both parties decide they want a relationship. They may not know the real reason they do ... they just feel it's time to find someone. If you're lucky, you *may* have an idea why that goes beyond hormonal activity. But my experience is that there isn't often a lot of clarity about exactly *why* we want a relationship other than being told by family and Hollywood that, like Van Halen once sang "Everybody Wants Some!" So once you've decided you want a relationship: (1) you meet someone; (2) you notice you're attracted to them; (3) you date for a while; (4) you add sex into the mix (often times, too soon); (5) if *that* all goes well, you decide you're going to date some more; and (6) at some point, you decide you both want to be in a committed relationship and continue down that track. If all *that* goes well, then it's not at all uncommon for cohabiting together to be next and—perhaps—marriage.

Along the way toward getting into a "committed relationship" with someone, you likely will have discussed your past relationship history with each other, some of what you like or don't like sexually, your past romantic history (if you have the guts and clarity to),

some of your family-of-origin history, and—maybe—
what your dreams are for your future on a professional
and personal level, to the degree you know them. What I
find perplexing is that, even with that whole sequence I
just laid out, the odds are slim that you'll have really
talked about how you want to design any relationship,
much less one with the person your heart (and other
parts) is convinced is *the one*! If you're like a lot of people
I've worked with, it's astonishingly easy to just go with
the feelings alone, trusting that you'll work shit out when
something goes wrong.

You see, one of the key reasons that relationships don't
seem to work (amongst many others) is that there's not
enough *up-front designing* being done going into building
a rock-solid foundation for the dream relationship you
really want to build. By "relationship and foundation
design," I'm referring to both of you talking about
fundamental things that you should *really* want to know
before committing to building a house or a long-term
relationship ... things like:

- Do you each know **why** you want a relationship to
  begin with?

- Why do you feel you're actually *ready* to have one
  at this particular point in time?

- Do you know what **purpose(s)** you ultimately
  want the relationship to serve, in *addition* to
  simply having companionship and sex (not that
  there's *anything* wrong with those, by the way!)?

- Do you know what's most likely to give you the
  best odds for a healthy relationship and what
  creates higher odds for failure?

- Who do you both really want this relationship to serve besides yourselves ... and how?

These are just a few of the many questions and elements that need to go into designing a conscious, Spirit-led relationship that has a foundation built to last. Here are some others I've discovered from all my couples clients over the years.

Real Adult Relationship or a Fairy-Tale Relationship

It's really important that you're totally clear on whether you want a real adult relationship or a fairy-tale one, like the ones you see in a lot of American movies. As an aside, let me point out that just asking a love partner that one question will open up a level of communication that will tell you SO much, such as how deep is this person, really? Unless you're looking for a shallow, disposable relationship, any kind of answer along the lines of "I don't know," or "Just because," are no-go's. If the other person says, "What a great question! I'd never thought about that," you've got real potential.

While there's a whole book that could be written just on "Real Adult Relationships: How to Have One with Your Head *Out* of Your Ass," let's just look at a few characteristics of what one of those really requires, so that you can know if it's something you're up for and/or ready to co-create.

The key, mandatory element of any truly adult, conscious relationship is a willingness and ability to see and feel things *just as they are*, rather than how you *wish* they were or would be. If you or your potential partner isn't able or willing to go there, your relationship is starting with a fundamental seismic crack in the foundation before you even really get started. Another variation of this is how much are you willing to *not* walk on eggshells? A lot of relationships start, understandably, with us putting on our best face and best persona because we've been conditioned to unconsciously default to the belief that we couldn't possibly be desirable just as we are. We want to impress, preen, seduce, and conquer. Much of this, in both genders, is biologically hardwired. The problem is that if we rely just on this biological imperative, as it were, we're seeing only what we want to see and what the other person wants us to see. The relationship between that and reality is often pretty different. (No wonder one of the most asked questions I get when couples come to see me to find out if their relationships can be fixed is, "What happened to the man/woman I fell I love with?")

Do you want to avoid Fairy Tale Land? Once you feel you're seriously attracted to someone, start asking the kinds of bold questions that will tell you just how ready you and your object of desire really are for a mature, adult relationship. Another way to find out whether your relationship can be well designed is to be brutally honest with yourself and the person you're interested in about how mature you want the relationship to be. If you're really brave and ballsy, you'll eventually want to share about how mature your *past* relationships have (or haven't) been. If you're both willing to be that vulnerable, especially early on, you have a much stronger shot at building a bulletproof foundation for your relationship.

This is a good time to point out that a big reason this is such an important thing to do in the early days of a relationship is that just about every couple I've ever worked with *didn't* do this kind of conscious legwork up front (or even when breakdowns started happening) ...

not because they were bad or unintelligent people, but because a lot of us weren't *taught* to do this kind of thing. We've been enculturated to believe that love is all we need and te rest will follow, like in the movies. Also, if we're not communicating with much depth and vulnerability, while maintaining an ever-present sense of curiosity, the chances are pretty high that that will continue over the duration of your relationship.

If you're not sure what the difference is between a mature and an immature relationship, you're going to want to know. Here are some key differences I've seen over the years (and the list could be even more exhaustive):

Immature Relationship Characteristics

- You expect your partner to meet a lot or all of your emotional needs.

- You expect your partner to be a certain way most of the time that makes you feel really comfortable.

- You depend on your partner to be able to "read" or know your emotional state the majority of the time and to proactively take care of it when it seems distressed (and should know how to do it).

- You feel that if you're providing enough financially, you've handled the majority of your responsibility or "workload" in the relationship.

- You believe that listening to your woman while you're reading your e-mail or texting someone is actually listening.

- You behave like an eight-year-old or a teenager when you're not getting your way, and you don't even realize it.
- You feel your hard work ethic, which is usually a somewhat thinly veiled workaholism and/or distraction technique, should be enough to prove to your woman that you're doing your part.

Mature Relationship Characteristics

- You make communication not only one of your highest priorities, but you do it especially when it's hard or frightening.

- You love your partner for who they are, and you are naturally driven to support them in bringing that out even more, without taking responsibility for it.

- When you can feel something's up with your woman, you ask, you really listen, and you don't accept "I'm okay" when every bone in your body tells you that isn't the truth.

- When something's up with you, you let your partner know early on in the distress instead of waiting until you *think* you've figured it out.

- You don't isolate yourself or each other. You both have a cadre of close friends that you empower to call you on your bullshit and reach out to when you need support. You support each other, yes, but you don't rely solely on each other for dealing with your stuff. Men need other men, and women need other women to lean into when the going's rough.

- When your woman has just given birth, you don't get pissed off when she doesn't want to let you anywhere near her Promised Land for a while.

- You don't try to guess what s/he needs, you ask. And you ask for what you need—clearly, succinctly, and compassionately. You practice vulnerability almost daily with each other, wanting support, but not expecting your partner to fix it for you.

Knowing *Who* You *Really* Want a Relationship With

This is *much* more than just finding the right person for you. It's actually even more important for you to be clear on this before you really start looking for someone. We think we're falling for a person we love. Again, we often confuse physical chemistry with true emotional chemistry (which gets easier to do, by the way, if we're really in a hurry to find someone [mayday!] and find ourselves believing that we can actually know we've found our life partner within just a few months or a few dates of getting acquainted with each other). What you *don't* know is how often the person that you *really* want a relationship with is actually going to be standing in for a parent, a grandparent, a sibling, Superman/Superwoman, or even your third-grade crush.

If you're thinking to yourself that I've lost my mind, and that there's no friggin' way you're looking for any of that … that you just want to have a great relationship with the future mother of your children … I'm here to tell you that you're full of it—without even realizing it, most likely. In leading over 300 workshops helping people heal family-of-origin wounds (and almost *everyone* gets wounded in their growing up years), studying what psychology terms attachment theory, and listening to over a thousand different/not-so-different stories from men and women alike, there is absolutely no question in my mind that the part of us that does the inner matchmaking and picks our partners is usually somewhere between five and ten years old ... no matter what our chronological age is. I've seen it over and over again.

Let me give you an example of what I'm talking about. Two of my clients, Bob and Shirley (not their real names) have been married for a few years, but they dated for several before they got married. Shirley had two kids (a boy and a girl) by her first husband who were young teenagers when Bob came into the picture. As their relationship progressed, there were a lot of tensions that rose between Bob and the boy. The boy was frequently irritating Bob, who loves this boy, but is perennially frustrated by him. This, of course, started creating a lot of friction between Bob and Shirley. Shirley often felt Bob was being too hard on the boy, and Bob felt Shirley was being too soft with the son. In digging down deep as to why this had become such an issue, we eventually came to see that Bob had grown up in rough circumstances where his mom loved him but had to work most of the time, leaving Bob to have to fend for himself at too young an age. Shirley had grown up feeling very unloved and unwanted by her mom; her dad loved her but seemed to prize intellectual achievement and debate skills over who Shirley actually was.

So, through the issues with the kids, several things became abundantly clear. A young part of Shirley, who'd grown up wanting more from her dad to help her feel loved and wanted in the face of a mother who made her feel exactly the opposite, had chosen Bob because he had the warmth and humor of an idealized dad and gave her a ton of nourishing verbal and sexual attention. Bob saw in

Shirley someone who was a great mom to her kids and , unconsciously, could provide nurturing maternal energy to him (which would be fine if Shirley was looking to be married to a son rather than husband). The situation with the kids brought up the fact that Bob would frequently get angry, jealous, and resentful of the son because when the son was doing things that were a problem for Bob, young Bob expected Shirley to essentially always choose him and take his side. When Shirley didn't do that, then Bob felt like a second banana, hurt, and angry. Bob, being a guy, handled this the way a lot of guys handle stuff: He didn't really tell the truth about how he was feeling, he isolated himself in work and electronic screens, and he kept telling Shirley (and me) that everything was fine. Shirley's daughter, however, often took sides with Bob, or at least gave Bob a lot of the affirmation and love that his little boy inside needed. That would often make Shirley feel resentful about Bob withholding himself from her while giving his heart to the daughter in a way that little Shirley had wanted so desperately when she was growing up. You getting the picture?

Both Bob and Shirley were in their mid- to late forties when they got together. Yet, unmet needs and wants from their childhood drove a part of their choice to be together and have been a key element in their conflicts and challenges ... all under the surface. When I first pointed this out to them, they couldn't get it. That was easy for me to understand because when our inner children (and I'm sorry to break it to you, but we all have 'em and they run the show 90–95 percent of the time) are driving the car of our partner selection and then the relationship itself, it's all happening unconsciously. It isn't that your adult self isn't healthily involved in your love and attraction to someone, but a big part of that will very likely be a function of an internal, child-aged Yenta. Once you can see that's what's going on, you can start changing habits, behaviors, and beliefs in such a way that your adult wisdom is running the show far more commonly.

Really Getting To Knowing Each Other

I work with couples all the time who've been together for years and are in breakdown because they never _really_ got to know about each other (and themselves) in the early stages of their relationship. So, this is critical to not overlook in the design phase of a relationship (though it's never too late or irrelevant, given we're always changing and growing, whether we like it or not).

It's crucial that—as you're getting to know each other _out_ of bed, too—you share your likes, your dislikes, your dreams, your hopes, your fears, what you wish for, and what you've already learned works and doesn't work about (and with) you in relationship, based on past experiences. You want to do that in a very honest, authentic, bold, and vulnerable way. In other words, you need to tell the whole truth, as best you know it, without falling prey to the common tendency of wanting to put your best foot and image forward. If you start the relationship with a carefully edited and presented persona and all the self-deceptive bullshit that usually goes with that, you start the relationship off with a level of incongruity and inauthenticity that will eventually come home to roost ... and starts a pattern that insidiously continues permeating your relationship.

A key part of this process – in both the design and maintenance phases of relationship - has to be a _lot_ of discussion and sharing about values. As I said in Section I, it's fine to have different values; however, if they're _too_ different ad/or just flat-out incompatible, you're going to have a very rough go of things, once things happen like no longer humping like rabbits every day, having to figure out how to integrate parenthood with your relationship, etc. You want to look at what they are, where they conflict, whether or not the conflicts seem manageable, and if there's a third set of values - the values for your relationship itself as an entity - that could be developed between the two of you that feel both doable and worth going for. These would be values you'd discover together that don't require either of you to give up who you are, but would allow you to be flexible enough to capitalize on your commonalities and your differences in a way that keeps you both sovereign while proactively charting new territory that grows you both.

You also want to spend time with each other's families and friends. Watching how your partner interacts with and relates to others they care about will tell you a lot! If you see things that concern you, things that feel like red flags, you've got nothing to lose and everything to gain in building a rock-solid foundation to share your concerns with each other, owning your concerns, and seeing what you both can learn and sort out in such a conversation. I read one blog post recently that also suggested that you should watch how your prospective partner treats wait staff, because the way they relate to servers in a restaurant has a surprising resonance with how they're likely to treat *you*. That makes sense, actually, if you believe (as I do) the adage of "How you do one thing is how you do everything," especially with that pesky 95 percent of the time being run by our unconscious patterns thing.

You want to notice how easy or hard it is to talk with each other in a vulnerable, heart-connected way. While there's a ton of room for anyone to change habits that don't serve them, it's important in the early stages of foundation design to know what baseline you're starting with, such as a guy who can't seem to offer up much more than "I don't know what I like," "I'm good," "Why do you want to talk about *that*?" or "I'm pretty easy with anything." Answers like those shouldn't necessarily send you running for the hills, but if that's really the best someone can come up with on a consistent basis, then a prospective partner has the right to know what some of the inner work is that will need to be an essential part of growing the relationship, sooner rather than later.

Suffice it to say that there's also a large burden on each of you to also be as *self*-aware as you can possibly be, especially when it comes to this kind of thing. If you've had several relationships, it would be wise for you to do your *own* inventory of what went wrong in those past relationships. What were the common issues that came up? How did *you* commonly react to and handle conflict in those relationships (or not)? What were the things with each partner that most pissed you off? When you can gather all that kind of information, then you can do the often uncomfortable work of looking at whether or not any of those things bear *any* similarity to:

- How one or both of your parents dealt with each other regarding conflict (or not)

- How one or both of your parents dealt with *you* in any way as you were growing up

- How you best got attention—positive or negative—growing up

- How you were rewarded with love in any way growing up

If you're finding a lot to connections there, you'll get a lot from Chapter 8, which will give you some guidance on what to do with those connections and insights.

It's a problem, too, that we don't really get much, if any, training or mentoring about how to really "screen" potential partners and people we've already begun falling for. So, I'm giving you an audio below on questions you can ask, and why, to see if you're really on a good road with someone.

http://www.builttolastbook.com/

<u>Knowing *Why* You Want a Relationship</u>

We're taught—as if it's a predestined eventuality—that teenagers and adults will fall in love, have relationships, and ultimately find Mr. or Mrs. Right. We're usually taught to follow our heart, and for teenage boys, it's not uncommon to confuse their sex drive for their hearts. What we're *not* taught often enough is to actually question ourselves *and* prospective partners on *why* we want to be in a relationship—and to question it at a depth that goes beyond just attraction—before getting in too deep, too quickly with someone. If you've already been a two-time (or-higher) loser in relationships, then it's definitely going to save you a lot of energy to explore this question.

What I'm really talking about here is to not ignore the huge importance of understanding what's *motivating* you to get into a relationship besides hormones and infatuation (not that those are bad, they're just not usually enough to build a life-lasting relationship foundation on). If you're "in between engagements," this is enormously wise proactive pain minimization. So, what exactly does that mean and look like?

Every human being's brain organizes life, input, data, conscious and unconscious responses, reactions, and things that seem like a crisis based on a lifelong web of beliefs, attitudes, values, and motivations that are all interwoven and often not always the exact same at any given time, in terms of what's the chicken and what's the egg. For purposes of this book, however, when talking about relationships, two of the most important things to focus on bringing from the unconscious to the conscious (if you want to be proactively building a rock-solid foundation for your relationship) are motivation and values. The two often have a very synergistic, relationship to and with each other.

Values are essential building blocks for motivation ... much more, in my experience, than the reverse.

For example, if a key *life* value for you is connection, and your conscious mind is telling you that a key motivation to be in a relationship is so that you're not the only one in your family that isn't, or that you're not the only bro in your social circle that hasn't been able to figure this out, you'd be going into a relationship with a pre-existing design flaw. Can you tell what it is? Here's the deal: in this example, you'd be going into something with an already existing values conflict. In addition to that little (which usually grows to a *big*) issue, you're also being motivated more by what you *don't* want than by what you do. And while being motivated by that isn't categorically a losing strategy, it'll likely get you short-term results you'll naively settle for ... and long-term dissatisfaction. Why? Because longer-term success is *far* more likely to be achieved when you are motivated toward what you want, rather than by what you're trying to avoid.

Think about it. How often have you felt burned out and dissatisfied by a particular job and said to yourself, "Screw this. I'm going to go get something much better," and then you actually did get a much better *paying* position ... and, within a year (at the most), you're sitting in the lunch room already bitching in your head about what's so unfulfilling. Or, for that matter (perhaps with a different timeline), you found yourself in that position regarding a relationship? In this job example, the key thing prompting you to take action is how unhappy you are in your current situation. In other words, you're motivated to reduce your suffering, not to increase your pleasure. Sure, there's *some* of that. But if you mostly just want to have your life *suck* less, you're caught in an away-from motivation strategy. Again, it can work for a while, but it's not as likely to stick over the long haul.

Imagine *this* scenario. You see an ad pop up on the Internet for a job in an area that you trained for because you were passionate about that particular subject and had been since you were a kid. However, you'd taken a better-paying job in a related but not exact-fit kind of field, and you'd built up an impressive resume in *that* field. Yet, great resume notwithstanding, you're bored shitless. So, you decide—even though it might seem like a long shot—to apply for it, because something in your gut is making you feel like you're *pulled* toward it. You actually get offered a job that feels great, gets you back in that field you wanted to be in when you were in high school and college ... but you're going to need to take a short-term salary cut. You decide to take it, because your gut's scooting you *toward* that passion. Within a year or two, you're happier with your career than you've been in years.

Can you see that, if you'd chosen a better-paying job like the one you were already unhappy with, *motivated* by wanting to get the hell out of Hell, that it wouldn't really have taken long before you were muttering under your breath, "Same old shit, different day!"?

One key element to avoid falling into these motivational traps, and the internal conflicts that tend to go with them, is to know *your* values at the very least. While this can be a very exhaustive process, I've included a relatively quick online assessment below that you fill out to begin seeing what your key relationship values are now (as opposed to when you were younger). When you see the results, it gives you a basis with which to begin exploring the same with your (prospective or actual) partner to discern both compatibility and conflicts that can seriously interfere with your long-term viability as a couple if kept in the dark.

http://www.builttolastbook.com/

So, here's one way to play with what I'm talking about within the realm of relationships (particularly if you're looking at starting a new relationship with someone). Grab a piece of paper and:

- Take a look at the last relationship you had (even before the one you may currently be in) that you once thought was the "perfect fit." Go back down Memory Lane, and write the top three to four things that really attracted you to that person.

- Write down three to four reasons you decided to go for having a relationship with that person, once you felt like you were in love with them (or at least liked them a lot).

- Then, look at each of those reasons and take into account the attraction elements and what was happening in your life at that time, and take a crack at determining if you were motivated by a towards motivation ... or an away-from motivation. You'll want to note that there are frequently elements of each that motivates our actions; but, you want to see what held the highest weight.

Now, for extra credit, do that same exercise for each of your past significant, high-commitment relationships (yep, even in high school), and see what patterns you notice. Then take a look at how your life—and each of these relationships—might've turned out if you and each of these past lovers could've been able to really know how to get clear on your "Why's?"—if you had done this exercise and compared notes. Whether you're in the early stages of a romantic partnership, or well into a committed relationship for several years, both of you should do this and share the "data" and how it hits you both. It can open up several great avenues of conversation that can deepen your emotional intimacy while also illuminating growth pathways for you both. If you're currently "in between engagements," this will help you better discern compatibility with a future relationship prospect.

It's useful to realize, by the way, that to have a great relationship, you don't both have to have *identical* values. You need to have *compatible*, complementary values. It can be both challenging and fun to discover what those might be. If you struggle with that and/or keep bumping into a lot of inner and outer conflict with each other on values, you'd be wise to get some help on this from a relationship coach/architect that is experienced in working with values from a rapid change context.

There's no question this can be some scary shit for both of you, particularly if you've already gone farther and faster than either of you would've imagined or predicted. But remember ... a foundation built upon how you *hope* something is or will be, versus how things actually *are*, is cracked before you ever put a bit of framing on it.

Chapter 3

Roles, Expectations, Needs, & Wants ... Oh MY!

Roles, Expectations, Needs, & Wants ...

Oh MY!

———————•●•———————

In all my years of working on relationships with people (most especially, their relationship with themselves first and with partners second) there's a mantra I've come to see should be taught to people in junior high at the earliest and in college (at the latest), along with why it matters and how to actually use it. It's the mantra that's the title of this chapter: "Roles, Expectations, Needs, & Wants ... Oh MY!"

Whether you're starting to design the foundation for a new relationship, or (re)designing a foundation for a brand-new version of a relationship or marriage you're already in, if you don't know what each of these means, how they're distinct, how they overlap, and how to work with them, you will have numerous potentially fatal relationship design flaws in that foundation. By the way, that essentially means that you're likely to be screwed ... and not in an enjoyable way.

Let's start by getting some basic, rule-of-thumb definitions going for each of the terms I work with most of the time.

Roles

It's incredibly valuable to realize, first of all, that every single one of us is, to some extent, playing one or more roles that we've carted along with us from our family of origin to every relationship we have. Some people, preferring a less complicated way of looking at things, would call this "the baggage we bring." Just like in a TV show, play, or film, "role" is defined as a character, a part, in that particular show, play, or film. Only when it comes to relationships, we're rarely aware of what role we've auditioned for (beyond the favored candidate to pursue *something* with), we don't know who's cast us (in a way, it isn't the man or woman who's picked you to date or get serious with, believe it or not), we don't have a printed script to memorize, we're not getting paid (in cash, anyway) to play the role(s) we're playing, we'll never be nominated for an Oscar or Tony for acting the role, and we'll rarely even get consciously acknowledged or appreciated for playing the role. We sure as hell won't get famous, or get an "Atta boy"; in fact, if you get an "Atta boy" for playing the kind of roles I'm talking about here, that's *rarely* a good thing.

The kinds of roles I'm talking about here include roles like:

- Caregiver
- Rescuer
- Neanderthal Man
- Oldest Child
- Middle Child
- Youngest Child
- Peacemaker
- Shit Disturber
- Dad

- Mom
- Passive-Aggressive Parent
- Aggressive-Aggressive Parent

... just to name a few.

Now, if you're looking at those and going "WTF?!" in your head, that's good. That means you still have hope! If you know what these really are and how you're playing any one of them - and you're still having the same relationship issues you've had in every other relationship - that means you're self-aware enough to effect change. If you're not aware of these (and are going "WTF?!"), then the odds are very high you're not that self-aware, but there's hope for you to learn, transform, and design a whole new way of being in a relationship, as well as co-designing a much higher quality foundation for the same.

We all (did you notice I said "All?") bring these and/or other such roles into every relationship we enter. Unless you've done some pretty deep inner work on yourself, you likely have little-to-no idea which of these roles (or others not listed) you're playing out and/or *how* you're doing it. A great deal of the neuroscience research of the last 10 to 20 years has consistently asserted that, if you want to know how much of the time you're operating and responding from your conscious mind (that rational, adult, compassionate part of you, along with your ability to think and process/analyze things that some people— myself included—refer to as "our adult self") well, it's about 5 percent. Yep, you read that right, people ... a meager 5 percent.

Well, if we're in our adult self only 5 percent of the time, what's running the show the other 95 percent of the time? As you may or may not be shocked to hear, it's the unconscious mind, and all the "programs" (as Dr. Bruce Lipton refers to them in his watershed *New York Times* best seller *The Biology of Belief*) contained therein. Dr. Lipton and fellow neuroscience guru Dr. Daniel Segal have both consistently stated that these "programs," along with energetic and behavioral patterns that go with them, start getting imprinted while we're in utero (the last month or two) up until we're about seven years old. So, until you know how to recognize and change these patterns, you can be a high-level corporate executive or a Steve Jobs, doing amazing things in the world while at work or at home, and you're being run most of the time by those fetal-to-about-seven-years-of-age parts of yourself, and probably not even aware how often you are … and HOW you are. Let me share a story by way of example.

When I was about thirty-four and still in the corporate world as a chief operating officer at an environmental consulting firm of high repute, I remember coming home one night and sitting down to dinner with Sarah (our son Marc, then aged seven, had already eaten and was off amusing himself elsewhere in the house). Sarah finished eating first and took her dishes to the sink while I sat finishing my meal. At some point while she was at the sink, Sarah asked me a very harmless question: "When you're done eating, would you empty the trash?" Now, that's truly a reasonable, benign request, asked with no discernible guile or ulterior motive of the treacherous kind. However, as soon as she said it, my internal emotional state went from zero to rage in about five seconds. I was so pissed. There was a barely detectable bit of adult, rational thinking I accessed along the lines of "Holy shit! Why are you getting so angry over this really simple thing?" (Sound familiar to you, by chance?) However, that oasis of rationality was short-lived and replaced by thoughts like, "WTF!" or "How dare she?!" or simple declarative thoughts like, "Fuck off."

Now, I *did* empty the trash, but I spent the next couple days not speaking to Sarah unless she spoke to me (though I wanted to even blow that off, but that ran counter to my peacemaker role that was burned into me as a kid by my mom and her mom). I didn't initiate conversation. I gave her looks that would kill (looks that I imagine bore a strong resemblance to "The Look" that my sister and I got from our mom when the shit was hitting the rotating equipment. I was very uncharacteristically monosyllabic when I *did* speak. I didn't even say "good night" when we went to bed. I kept waiting for her to come and apologize and ask me what was wrong. I waited for a while (while she was waiting for me to get my head out of my butt and grow up), without so much as an olive branch or "What's wrong, honey?"

"Jesus H!" I thought to myself. "What's she *waiting* for?"

Fast-forward to a week or two later, and I have this epiphany (thanks to a coach I was working with back then) that (1) it wasn't the question or request itself, (2) it was Sarah's tone of voice that had actually created such a strong response, and (3) it sure as hell was not my then thirty-four-year-old self that blew the inner gasket. As it all became clear, I was able to see what had happened, and that my response came from an inherent role I brought to *all* my relationships that conflicted with adult reason. In my family growing up, the dominant role I was trained to play was peacemaker. It was *my* job—and mine alone—to make sure that everyone in the family was happy at best and, at worst, wasn't pissed off or upset. So, right off the bat, a conflict emerged between that peacemaker part (or role) of me—for whom the prime directive (if you're not a Trekkie, I hope you understand that term) was to never have someone pissed off or upset (first), or anyone else (when the first one was settled) for that matter. So, imagine the bind I was in, being so furious but unable to express that, rational or not (and this was not a rational experience for me that night). My pattern, my program, and my role was to observe the prime directive, no matter what feelings and needs were there!

To wrap up the story in a way that helps you turn this into both an explanation and a tool for getting yourself out of your 95 percent when YOU'RE unintentionally making an ass out of yourself, the key question becomes, "What to do?"

When I figured out that it was Sarah's tone of voice, not the request itself, I started to figure out what exactly it was about her tone that blew my inner lid off. It didn't take long to see that, even though Sarah's voice was *very* different from my mom's, in that particular moment, it was close enough to Mom's that I *immediately* shifted to being about fifteen years old inside (that would be the "Fuck off" part).

Then, the next "A-ha" was that the part of what Sarah asked that got me so cheesed off (otherwise referred to as "the content" of what she said) wasn't really about emptying the garbage, it was about the *timing*. You see, when I was a young kid, another big role that I was expected to play (and play well) was being my mom's little manservant. One of the things that I can remember absolutely enraging me as a kid was my mom's habit of giving me two to three things to do, and whilst I was still in the midst of doing the first thing, she'd often give me two or three more to do ... while I was still on the first one! Nothing (to this day) could overwhelm me more than that kind of thing. So that night, Sarah sounded like my mom and asked me to do something in a way (because of its timing) that came off as replicating one of my mom's most upsetting habits.

Once I figured that out, I was able to see just how much Sarah had simply stepped into the wrong moment the wrong way at the wrong time (not that there would've really ever been a "good" time), and I'd gone ballistic, becoming that fifteen-year-old frequently caught in a conflict between that peacemaker part of me and the teenager who wanted to tell his mom to fuck off on more than one occasion, to put it mildly. (I'm sure it's become apparent that, like many men, I had serious "Mom" issues and conflicts.)

But, the teaching (and example) doesn't stop there. There's no question that, if you can "catch" yourself playing one of the roles you had modeled for you (my business coach, Ronda Wada, uses a great distinction: "Is it your truth, or just your training?"), you have the power—by just sheer force of will, at worst—to stop everything dead in its tracks and make a different choice about how to respond to an upset. You could say we're virtually neurologically hardwired to defer to the most dominant roles. However, I didn't know that that night.

When I looked even more deeply into my mind and my gut, I had this other realization. Some of our roles have other roles that support *them*. In this case, the role (or "part") that jumped in for the best performance by a supporting actor was my mom! Not my physical mom, but the energy and behavior of my mom that had driven me batty for about thirty years and that I didn't even see I was bringing out on several occasions to try to resolve a conflict. So, in this particular example, the mom part came out and did to Sarah *everything* that I most hated having done to me by my mom growing up or beyond ... an intense passive-aggressiveness: "The Look," icing someone out, fuming without saying anything while expecting the harmless victim to atone and take care of *my* fragile state, etc. (anything except simply communicating the upset, resolving it, and moving on). Put another, more humbling way, Sarah triggered me into an old, unresolved issue with Mom, which really pissed me off, and then I handled it by *doing* my mom! Again, I say,, "WTF?!!" Yet, some version of this is going on in each relationship we have that's in any way consistent and meaningful to us.

In designing a really strong relationship foundation, you really want to know:

- The key roles you're bringing

- How they show up (good, bad, and ugly)

- What seems to consistently trigger such roles for you and in your partner/p partner [If you want a great practice to develop this skill, by the way, sit in a business meeting and just watch how old people are at any given time and what roles/parts they then automatically and unconsciously take on—and the roles all the others in the meeting start enacting in response.)

- How to get "un-triggered" and back to yourself before you do any kind of real damage

The roles you bring to the party are not ones you're permanently stuck with. They are your opportunities to free yourself of family lineage that doesn't serve your happiness and to discover—with your partner or a future partner—who you really are that you can get excited to bring to a love relationship in ways you never have.

Expectations

Do you know the definition of "expectation"? If you don't, why not?! I *expect* you to at your age, for crissakes!

Now, just look at how you first reacted to that opening statement ... how it made you feel. If it was annoying in any way, or if it even flat-out pissed you off, or made you shrink or pull in your energy in *any* way, you can immediately see the power expectations can (and probably often do) play in your relationships.

In Webster's Dictionary, there are four different definitions of "expectations," but there are two of them that frequently play out and cause problems in relationships:

1. "The act or state of expecting: anticipation <in *expectation* of what *could* happen (in relationships, "What could" usually gets changed to "What *should* happen); and

2. Something expected <not up to expectation><expectations for a recovery after one has made a fool of themselves>

Now, expectations in and of themselves aren't always "bad." It is crucial have a lot of clarity on them, though, while building a relationship foundation because while new expectations always pop up along the Marital Highway, the ones you don't talk about, share, and explore in the early stages of things are almost always the ones that will likely cause cracks in the foundation along the way, the ones that will eventually bite you in the ass. For that matter, the ones you don't ever talk about at any point in your relationship will come back to bite you on the butt.

I'll be crystal clear here. While I think it's best to keep expectations in relationships to a minimum, they're gonna happen, on both sides. So, a way to turn potential foundation cracks into great foundation glue, once you're both clear that you're getting serious about a long-term relationship with each other, is to do the following:

- Take your own personal inventory of what was expected of you when you were growing up, and what's expected of you now. You'll likely notice that there is some degree of overlap between past and present.

- Set a timer for fifteen minutes, and do a totally stream-of-consciousness data dump of what your expectations are of relationships in general and any person that you'd likely hook up with for more than a few hot dates. Then, within a day or two, do the exact same thing in retrospect. In other words, if you look at your past serious romantic relationships you've had that didn't make it, see if you can retroactively recreate what your expectations of each former partner were. Be specific. Then, compare all the lists against each other and see what patterns and similarities you notice—particularly, what you see with your past relationship expectations and what was expected of you as a kid. Pay particular attention to how many of the aforementioned expectations were ever even consistently communicated to your exes (or to your current partner, for that matter, if you have one).

- Set aside time with your honey (it would be wise to invite them to do the same exercise) to share what you each came up with—not just the lists themselves, but also your observations, intuitive insights, and any awarenesses you gained. Then, be sure to brainstorm together on what you can each do about proactively anticipating and working through problems and conflicts.

One parting thought on expectations: Again, they're *going* to show up. Yet the biggest differentiator between constructive & useful vs. toxic & destructive expectations is communicating them ... transparently, vulnerably, and authentically (see Chapter 10 in Section II on communication). It won't hurt to also examine which expectations you're carrying are realistic and unrealistic. Many people have unrealistic expectations (e.g., "I expect my partner to read my mind and know my emotional state and needs without me having to tell them!")

It's also really helpful to get intimately familiar with expectations' first cousin: *assumptions*. Oh boy! How often have you found yourself on the receiving end of some seriously hostile attitude from someone because you didn't do something that was expected of you, it was assumed that you'd be doing whatever it was, and yet you had no friggin' idea about either! To be fair, how often have *you* been on the *giving* end of the metaphorical slap down on your friend, partner, or co-worker because of assumptions you may not have even been consciously in touch with having? That sound familiar at all?

Here's an example of what I'm talking about: Elizabeth (again, not her real name) would often go into a slow burn whenever Don (nor his real name) would spend any money on things that really brought him pleasure. Now, Don had grown up in a family where money was abundant, the energy around it in the house was relaxed, and there hadn't been any noticeable tension. Elizabeth, however, had grown up in a poor family, where everything was lack-filled and lack-based, and anxieties often ran high around money. So, even though she knew that—between them—they grossed nearly a million a year, whenever he came home with a $100-500 "toy," she'd find herself feeling some blend of irritation, fear, and anxiety; she just wouldn't communicate either the reaction or what was underneath it. First, because she didn't want to upset Don (you'll read more about co-dependence in Section III), and second because she wasn't really even conscious of it! What Elizabeth wasn't seeing (Don sure kept feeling it coming from her energetically though) was how much deep resentment she had unconsciously stored from that young part of her—that part that was often deprived of what *she* wanted as a kid—that *expected* her Prince Charming to provide and assumed that Don would, but that also assumed that Don would be thrifty, that he would *know* to be that given her background (even though she'd only told him half the story of how bad it really was for her), and that he would just get in some kind of lockstep with her. Until we got down to this discovery in our work together, she had no idea she was carrying these assumptions and expectations and was just dumbfounded at why her reactivity was so high when he'd spend (relatively) small amounts of money that they clearly *could* afford.

Wants & Needs

One of the biggest problems that pops up in relationships is that people often confuse wants with needs. To make matters worse, women have largely been conditioned to order short, or settle, when it comes to their needs (including what they can and can't do with their bodies). Many of the men of my generation and the ones before were conditioned to consider things like needs, wants, vulnerability, and feelings as signs of weakness at worst, and frivolous—or something to fit in when you can—at best. For guys, at our most unconscious levels, it seems as if it's okay to have wants and that the most socially acceptable wants should involve sex, money, sports, and/or cars. So it's no wonder that these two things end up getting pretty confused.

On the surface, you'd think the differences would be pretty self-evident. Yet I've run into situations with marriages where the couple's financial situation is very tight, so tight that they have to decide whether to get store-brand toilet paper or the "premium" brand, just to save 40 cents. Yet, in spite of that, the husband—who's not fully happy with his work and knows, deep inside, that he can't tolerate it much longer (hence, creating a great threat to "security")—comes home one night and tells his wife he's interested in getting a luxury car. He actually tells her he needs a new car because it will present a higher-level image ... and because he "needs" a new car. Oh yeah ... and they still have over a year to pay on their current car until it's paid off.

Okay ... so what's wrong with *that* picture?

Take another marriage, one where—like the previous example—money's really tight. A situation arises where the wife begins noticing that she's got some health stuff going on. She's getting a lot of sore throats, feeling lethargic a lot, having trouble focusing at work, lowered energy and libido, and a lot of weight gain. She can feel that *something's* not quite right with her body. Yet she's not really telling her husband and kids the full truth about what's going on because she knows that going to the doctor is going to cost some money. She puts it off because she knows her husband gets distressed about money, no matter how much they have (or don't have). So she labels it, in her mind, as a want when her body's actually trying to help her get that it's actually a need. Something's wrong here (which is what turned out to be the case, by the way).

Now, here's a rub: There are basic human needs that we all have. Yet our minds are developed enough that we can easily override our energy and our bodies and just power through or over our needs. So, in the Spirit of designing and building the best possible foundation for a relationship, you have to:

- Get oriented on (even if you think you already know them) what the basic human needs are. I still think that the best and most basic breakout of what those are remains Abraham Maslow's *Hierarchy of Needs: A Theory of Motivation*, written in 1943. Is it the exhaustive and definitive treatise on needs? No. Is it flawless and airtight? NO! However, there's a strong reason that it's still studied to this day: it's close enough for government work! One other thing about this ... it's also wise to know/remember that basic needs such as connection, touch, intimacy, and relationships of multiple sorts—just to name a few—are indeed needs, not airy-fairy whims or esoteric bullshit.

- Bone up on attachment theory and how it came to be developed. The chapter in this book entitled, "Just How Many People Are You Really Sleeping With" elaborates on why having a basic knowledge of the key concepts and examples of how attachment theory translates into "reality" can save you a ton of heartache and a good chunk of change.

- You have to know what, *in addition* to Maslow's Hierarchy of Needs, *your* particular, unique, and non-negotiable *needs* are. These are the things that you're just not willing and able to do without, things such as integrity, accountability, a certain level and amount of touch, honesty, directness, presence—just to name a few possibilities that might fit for you. If you're not sure what your needs are, let me tell you that you actually probably do, but you can't remember the last time you gave yourself permission to have them. If you really can't believe yet that you know what they are, then look at what consistently pisses you off, makes you go away, and makes you feel powerless/hopeless. On the other side, you'll find what you need.

- Lastly, share all the above with your partner (and they, of course, should do the exact same exercise). In a very bold show of inner strength and resolve to have a relationship built on authenticity rather than trying to *look good*, you two should then take a fair amount of time (not all in one sitting) to discuss them in depth. Be honest with each other about how you feel about each other's lists (without judgment, to the extent humanly possible). Share what you're happy to see, what scares you, what turns you off, recognizing that it's not up to either of you to change anything, but to identify potential design flaws up front that allow you both the room to proactively decide what you each can flow/bend with and what you can't ... and if the things you can't are deal breakers.

Overall, a key thing you must do in designing your relationship up front (and in an ongoing manner, once you're going through the years in your relationship) is to be as crystal clear and honest about your needs with yourself and each other. As you do so, you also need to be willing to not only examine any hidden agendas in the needs—and unhide them—but to also be able to individually and collectively prioritize the needs (and wants) that are most important to nurture and fulfill.

If you take the time to do that with each other and really be fearless in it, then you're giving your relationship a much stronger foundation to build on. If you're already in a long-term relationship, this actually gains even more importance because wants, needs, and values change along with each of us, and with time. That will be discussed much more in Section II.

Chapter 4

Spiritually or Ego-Centered Relationship?

Spiritually or Ego-Centered Relationship?

Many couples that have come to see me for help in getting "the love" back into their relationship share similar stories. The details are different, of course, but the "issue" is pretty similar. What they're sharing with me is that they are in a lot of conflict, their sex life is virtually nonexistent, and they snipe at each other a lot. They hide behind their parental responsibilities, they don't even really know how to talk to each other beyond the surface stuff, and they often can't pinpoint where things went south. They just know that there's now a chasm between them that's getting unbearably painful.

There are lots of reasons why this kind of relationship emerges from what started as love, a desire to be together all the time, and feeling so tuned into each other's hearts, minds, and bodies. This chapter addresses one prominent reason that this happens, and it's usually indicative of a relationship design flaw that occurred in the foundation design stage ... or that didn't have a chance to form, because there really *wasn't* a design stage. That reason is that there weren't any up-front conversations about whether each of you were looking for a Spiritually centered relationship or an ego-centered one. Because neither of those distinctions were ever pointed out or taught to me in high school or college, I'm guessing it didn't happen for you, either. It's easy to see, then, how this gets missed. However, it no longer needs to be.

Let's start by defining the qualities and characteristics of each kind of relationship, after first pointing out that *no* relationship is absolutely one or the other, nor can it be. We're human beings with egos, so there's virtually no way to avoid the presence of ego relationship qualities in your relationship, but if there's a stronger bent toward designing and building a Spiritual—or Spirit-led—relationship as a top priority, then challenges and struggles generated from each person's ego can have a better shot at being resolved more quickly and with less collateral damage.

Ego Relationship

Let's start with what I mean by "ego." We all have egos. We couldn't function without one. We all have one brain, but two minds: the conscious mind and the subconscious mind. A great analogy is that our brain is like our internal hard drive, and our mind is the operating system and software. You can look at the conscious mind as if it's what you see on your computer screen, and the unconscious mind often determines what you're typing that shows up on the screen. Put another way, your conscious mind is the captain of your ship, and the unconscious mind is the crew of the ship making the ship go wherever the captain orders it to go ... or not. For this book, I'm simplifying ego into two different *aspects* of ego: (1) healthy ego (which is mostly the conscious mind), and (2) the shadow ego, which is largely in the unconscious mind. I mentioned earlier in the book the startling scientific finding (at least to me) that most human beings spend only about 5 percent of the time running their lives from their conscious minds. You don't have to be a math genius to figure out that that means 95 percent of the time, on average, we're all running around living our lives driven by unconscious programming, which isn't all "bad" or shadow. A lot of it, though, is programming that was already in place in our subconscious by about the age of seven and includes energy patterns that were getting into our heads (and bodies) as early as the third trimester of our being in utero.

An acronym for shadow ego that I like is **E**dging **G**od **O**ut. Now, understand that I'm not using the word "God" in any theological or religious way. It's a term used for whatever Higher Power you may believe in, and if you don't believe in any kind of Universal or Higher Power, you can look at it as referring to *your* Spirit, that part of you that will leave your body when you take your last breath. Simply put, this part of the ego believes that it knows more than your Spirit or God, and it can do a much better job of running your life than your Spirit ever could ... especially in the face of clear evidence to the contrary regularly being demonstrated in how your life seems to be going.

The healthy ego is the part of us that is truly the best possible servant of our heart and Spirit. For example, when we get really clear input from our own Spirit that we're supposed to be doing X, and—in spite of the other part of our ego's protests to the contrary—there's not a shadow of a doubt about it, the healthy ego will come up with ways that it can happen ... ideas, strategies, tactics, and specific actions for forwarding things along, just to name a few. When you realize you're falling for someone, the healthy ego will help devise and execute ideas for wooing the object of your affection.

The reality is that, in *every* relationship we have, healthy ego and shadow ego always come into play. This isn't about trying to design a relationship where your shadow doesn't pop up, or where you're always floating above the clouds in Nirvana, oblivious to what it's like to be grounded in third-dimensional consciousness that we need to function in day-to-day life. It's about figuring out how to design a relationship that takes the shadow into account (and even invites it out) but consistently prioritizes finding and expanding what the healthy ego can bring when used in concert with your Spirit's (or your Higher Self, if you will) knowing and direction.

Before defining distinct qualities of an ego-centered relationship, it's useful to remind you that how you experience your life every day has everything to do with what you *actually* experience (not the shit you make up in your head, and we all make up plenty of that!), combined with how you *interpret* your experience, how you *relate* to that interpretation, and how you *manage* all the above. Notice how often in that last sentence I used the word "you"? That's because I can't stress enough how much designing a conscious relationship—and then building, living, and maintaining it—is an inside job. If you can design your relationship foundation in full agreement with your partner that there are *no* exceptions to this, that only *each* of you are creating your experience— regardless of circumstances—you'll build and maintain a much stronger, healthier, and conscious relationship for years. Here are some qualities of an ego-centered relationship that incorporate both healthy and shadow ego aspects (see if you can guess which is which):

- It's usually about *you* and believing you should be happy all the time, and that your partner should live for nothing but seeing that that happens, regardless of their needs and wants.

- You're able to think about and place your attention on the well-being of others more than occasionally.

- Your measures of success for the relationship tend to be more quantitative than qualitative (e.g., material measures, how much sex you're having or not, your financial situation, status, etc.)

- Goals and visions you set for the relationship have little emotional and Spiritual content.

- One or both of you want frequent or continual stimulation; in other words, you get bored easily in the relationship and believe it should be exciting and highly stimulating most of the time.

- If you have children, you put them first over yourself and the health of your relationship (more on that in Section III).

- You both believe the purpose of the relationship is mostly to make you both happy, and you have conscious and/or unconscious beliefs that—if your relationship is successful—living happily ever after will be the inevitable and desirable outcome.

- You find yourselves keeping score regarding how much you've given versus what your partner's been giving, and the relationship subtly (or not so subtly) becomes a competition. To see an exaggerated (but not wholly inaccurate) version of what I'm talking about, watch the movie *The War of the Roses.*

Spiritual Relationship

To put it really simply, what I refer to as "Spiritual Relationship" is when both parties realize that their relationship is a gift from Spirit, serves Spirit, is served by

Spirit, and that you both return to each of your Spiritual purposes/missions when the going gets tough (and it does in *every* relationship, sooner or later).

I invite you to imagine and visualize a triangle with the word "Spirit" at the top of the triangle. Then, imagine your name and your partner's name on the two bottom corners of the triangle. In this model of Spiritual relationship—or a term I like even better is "Spirit-led relationship"—both people recognize that what sources (or empowers) their relationship is each of their individual connections to and relationships with the divine/their Spirit, which they then share with each other back and forth on the bottom line of the triangle. Then, for those with children, as Spirit sources each of you, you get to feed and empower the well-being of your kids from that.

So, in other words, a Spirit-led relationship is really one where each person, and the relationship, is guided—first and foremost—by each person's commitment to consistently connecting with their heart and their Spirit, to the best of their abilities, and allowing their relationship to be an "out-picturing" of both that commitment and the results of that commitment. Here are some qualities that characterize a Spirit-led relationship:

- Having (and doing) Spiritual practices are a key value for each of you within the relationship.

- You both consciously acknowledge—to yourselves and each other—that you're choosing to use your relationship as a fast-track to your spiritual growth. If this is in place foundationally, then when conflict erupts, you're far less likely to just bail.

- You choose to interpret challenges not as problems but as opportunities your Spirits are giving you to keep evolving you and the relationship.

- You realize you can't even go to scorekeeping because you recognize that—Spiritually—no one is better than anyone else and that the relationship is about living as sacred love, not winning a competition.

- It becomes second nature to place connection (to each other, to your own Spirits, and to your hearts) above being right. You treat each other like the Beloved (or however you envision the Divine Itself). That means, for example, that no matter how angry you may be, you don't talk to your partner differently than you would talk with Spirit if it were sitting in your living room having a conversation. [Through all the decades I've been with Sarah I have never said, "Fuck you" to her, even at my angriest ... just to give you a concrete example of what I'm talking about here.]

While there are many more characteristics and forms of Spirit-led relationship, these are enough to get you started in the design phase of a relationship that's built to last. The key thing is to be mutually aligned with the goals of (1) deciding which of these two types of relationships most calls to you both, and (2) then devoting the time to consciously lay out some concrete ideas about how you're going to set up foundational agreements and principles that you commit to living with each other that serve the best of each of these kinds of relationships, while also accounting for the reality that the shadow ego will resist and act out ... and that you're going to support each other when they do by loving that part of your egos into submission.

To hear more about my take on ego-centered and spiritually centered relationships, I'm happy to share an audio interview I did recently on this subject, which you can access by clicking on the link below.

http://www.builttolastbook.com/

Chapter 5

Choreographing the Dance of Emotional and Physical Intimacy

Choreographing the Dance of Emotional and Physical Intimacy

While I address intimacy in a more pragmatic way in Section III, it's important—as we're looking at how to optimize designing an incredibly durable and resilient foundation for a relationship that's truly built to last—to touch on the role of intimacy in the relationship design phase of things.

It's no wonder that intimacy can be so hard to define, given that Webster's definition doesn't offer anything more than: "the state of being intimate: familiarity," and "something of a personal or private nature." When it comes to "relationship," things get a bit clearer when you look at the Webster synonyms for "intimacy": "belonging, chumminess, closeness, inseparability, familiarity, nearness." Ironically, other than intimacy's frequent association with sex, if you went by the dictionary definition, it would seem that intimacy is about privacy, which is the exact opposite of what's going to help optimize the durability of your relationship in the design, building, and maintenance stages of your built-to-last relationship. Where things get really juicy is when you use intimacy as another way of saying, "extremely close, deep, and not-so-private."

Based on my participating in and/or leading over 500 men's meetings over the last 15 years, intimacy can be challenging for the average guy when so many of us are conditioned to just say "fine" or "good" when asked how we're doing, how's life, how's things with your relationship, and how are things going at work. It's also easy to just jump to the assumption that men are taught to be emotionally shut-down or guarded because that's "how men are supposed to be." Ascribing men's challenges with intimacy (and the stereotypes around that) to the simple fact that they're men has *some* validity. (There *are* many, many decades of reinforcement behind the idea that, for men, sharing feelings is weak and will hurt you.)

However, in over 30 years of observing and working with men and women, in and out of relationship contexts, I've come to see that intimacy issues are less gender issues than they are *human* issues. Neither gender has a lock on how to be intimate or how not to be. I believe that designing, building, and maintaining your dream relationship gets a hell of a lot easier when you start the design part of things with a lot of discussions about what you each think intimacy is, what it isn't, how you relate to the concept at all (or not), how you think and feel you show intimacy, how you know you repel and deflect from giving/receiving intimacy, ways you distract yourself from it, and how much you hold intimacy as a key value. These kinds of conversations really need to happen periodically throughout the life of a relationship, but they are extremely important to have in the early stages of designing a relationship (which is to say, the first year or two).

So, let's look at some key distinctions and definitions—practical, common sense distinctions at that—for physical and emotional intimacy. And, by the way, as you read on in this chapter, be sure to pay close attention to any feelings in your body that come up as you do. Your mind will likely have all kinds of thoughts about this stuff, but your body and feelings are what you want to pay attention to because that will tell you way more about how you relate to intimacy in general and where your growth opportunities lie.

Physical Intimacy

Okay, for you guys reading this (and you women, too), this may seem like it's so self-evident as to be ludicrous for me to even have this in here. If you were between fifteen and twenty-two or so, that would make perfect sense. However, with no offense to people in that age bracket, if you're reading this book, it's because you're tired of allowing those (inside) parts of you that are that age or younger to be in charge of your love life, aren't you?

Of course, physical intimacy relates to sex, but all aspects and shades of sex, not just the "old in-out," as the character of Alex in *A Clockwork Orange* would say. Anyone can fuck. It's simple mechanics, it feels good, it has a very worthwhile place in life, but that's not what I'm referring to. I'm talking about *everything* that leads to conscious sex, things like connecting intellectually and emotionally before intercourse ever happens. When you're really feeling into someone you're attracted to (or your already existing partner), the first part of intimate sex begins in the eyes, making yours a true doorway to your soul and using the other person's to give you a glimpse into who they are in that moment. When you remember that the two biggest sex organs (sorry guys) in every human is the brain and the entire epidermis (otherwise known as skin), this makes perfect sense.

Physical intimacy starts with *connecting* somehow, and eyes and simple touch are a key part of it.

Another aspect of physical intimacy is teasing—verbally, non-verbally, tactilely, and through seductive clues that lead your partner to imagine what's going to ensue. This is a great way to bring the mind into physical intimacy, along with fantasy, role-playing, blindfolds, and any other number of ways to be intimate without any genital contact at all that's just as intimate as intercourse. I also want to suggest that physical intimacy is not about orgasms. (Don't get me wrong—I'm a *big* fan of those!) We have placed way too much emphasis on the orgasm, versus the intimacy, being the brass ring with sexuality, particularly among the young who don't know better yet. Intimacy, in general, wouldn't have any competitive or goal-oriented factor. If either of you are focused on achieving/giving The Big O, you're may get there, but at the cost of achieving a Big Dud when it comes to true, emotional intimacy potential.

Another key part of physical intimacy is affection. There will be many times where, for a variety of reasons, sex may not be possible or even remotely desired, but affectionate touch, with no ulterior motive other than to physically connect and love on your partner, can go a long way toward keeping you both physically intimate when sex is taking a backseat for whatever reason and you're both waiting to bring it back to the front seat.

In the design phase, you want to really explore as many facets of physical intimacy as you can. If you have no sexual chemistry (including the hormonal euphoria and horniness that comes in the early stage of any relationship), that's going to be an issue for quite awhile (though not automatically unresolvable, in my opinion).

Another great opportunity is to explore the intimacy that comes with communicating about sex before, during, and after ... about what you want, what you like, what you don't like, what you want to do to your partner, what you can't wait for them to do to you. Those kinds of things should be basic, but it's disturbingly common for me to hear how little gets said about and in sex within a relationship.

Again, physical intimacy is wonderful, in and of itself; however, if you add emotional intimacy to it, it goes to another dimension that many people can't imagine. So let's explore emotional intimacy next.

Emotional Intimacy

Emotional intimacy really starts when you reconfigure the word "intimacy" to "into-me-see." It all starts with how intimate you're willing to be with yourself—kinda like the old chestnut (however true), "You can't love someone else any more than you love yourself." To really love yourself, you have to *know* yourself—the good, the bad, and the ugly—and embrace it all. This is no easy feat, but it's essential. My assertion is that to really do that— and to have a thriving, long-term relationship—you have to be willing to be emotionally intimate with *yourself* first and foremost. That means you have to be cool with and committed to what Plato called "the Examined Life."

This is *not* to say, by the way, that you're analyzing and trying to figure out the meaning of every damn thing in every moment. That just leads you *away* from emotional intimacy. I'm talking about being *committed* to periodic self-examination and introspection balanced with really being present as much as you can in each current moment. Let me put it another way: if you've never done any inner work on yourself and your partner hasn't either, your relationship will not have the strongest foundation it can have. If you and your partner subscribe to the belief that you each should be able to figure out most problems or issues on your own for the duration of your marriage, you're likely to have a shorter duration than you planned (more on this in Section III). A willingness to see that relationship, again, is the fastest track to personal and Spiritual evolution will beautifully pave the way to a huge treasure trove of emotional intimacy.

Another element of emotional intimacy is being committed to the V word (and I'm still not referring to the V word that might pop into your mind): *vulnerability*. A relationship without vulnerability on both sides is going to fail, whether you keep living together or not. In her great book, *The Gifts of Imperfection: Let Go of Who You Think You're Supposed to Be and Embrace Who You Are*, Dr. Brene Brown says, "Vulnerability is the birthplace of innovation, creativity, and change." She also captures such a core truth about love and intimacy when she says:

> We cultivate love when we allow our most vulnerable and powerful selves to be to deeply seen and known, and when we honor the Spiritual connection that grows from that offering with trust, respect, kindness, and affection. Love is not something we give or get; it is something that we nurture and grow [through emotional and physical intimacy], a connection that can only be cultivated between two people when it exists within each one of them. Shame, blame, disrespect, betrayal, and the withholding of affection damage the roots from which love grows.

> Love can only survive these injuries if they
> are acknowledged, healed, and rare.

Another characteristic is connection—emotional, physical, mental, and Spiritual/heart connection. In my experience, connection is nearly impossible to have and sustain without vulnerability. This includes, by the way, a vulnerability that isn't just about being willing to be fully transparent, but includes your willingness to let your guard down enough to truly let love in. A lot of guys think of vulnerability as "spilling your guts" or "contemplating my navel." It *is* about that, but it's also about letting in more joy, fun, and pleasure than you've ever allowed yourself to have ... with and without your partner.

Emotional intimacy and vulnerability come from truly treating and relating to your partner as your best friend. It's about sharing when you feel overwhelmed, sharing your fears, sharing your wins/celebrations, sharing your dreams and vision, sharing your insecurities, sharing your presence, and encouraging the same from your partner as both a regular practice and a way of being with life.

As you're in the stage of designing your relationship foundation, this all has to be discussed. You want to share as much as you each dare about your feelings and thoughts about intimacy and vulnerability. Where have they bitten you on the ass in the past ... and why? How do you tend to protect yourself from being too intimate? (And what IS too intimate for you, by the way?) Talk about what your favorite ways of being emotionally and physically intimate have been in the past, and how you want to see all that shift going forward in a new relationship. If you're in a long-term marriage that needs to be redesigned and reinvented, these same questions are just as important now because you're not the same people you were when you started out in the relationship.

Lastly, it's going to be very helpful for your relationship to see if you can both be on the same page believing that neither physical nor emotional intimacy is better than the other. We need them both; however, if you mostly lead from a commitment to emotional intimacy, the payoff will be much richer and broader and lead to infinitely better physical intimacy.

Section II

Laying the Foundation and Building the House to Last

———————•◆•———————

If you have taken to heart the reasons and ways for consciously designing a rock-solid foundation for your built-to-last relationship (And, *why would you not want to do that?*), and you and your partner have gotten clear through that process that you're both committed to going forward, then it's time to start actually laying the foundation and building what you want to have last a lifetime.

In this section, I'm going to cover several of the considerations, specific issues, and ways to build a truly, passionate, loving, lasting, and conscious relationship. Know up front that this is not meant to be the exhaustive reference manual on how to *do* relationship right. Rather it's filled with information that you'll both relate to and recognize as areas that you've run into before (or most certainly will, at some point).

My intent is that you can use the material in this section in real-life, pragmatic ways; however, *pragmatic* doesn't mean you won't have to stretch yourself emotionally, mentally, physically, and Spiritually. Relationship exists as a pathway to our own human and Spiritual evolution. In my fifty-seven years thus far, I've come to see that the best growth and evolvement require a blend of learning, practicing, and stretching myself; dealing with what I've avoided dealing with for decades; being vulnerable; and holding the whole shooting match as an adventure, not as the existential equivalent of a root canal. Embrace the process, don't rush it, stay patient and persistent, embrace the team partnership elements, try what's in here, and you'll reap the rewards. Be the tortoise, not the hare. Most importantly, remember that you're not striving for The Perfect Relationship ... it doesn't exist. If you're reading this book, you're striving for the best relationship you can co-create with your partner and your Spirit that will endure and grow with you both; in other words, go for a perfectly imperfect relationship ... it's much more fun!

Some of the topics that we'll cover in this section include control (not that that's important to you, I'm sure), avoiding living with an "invisible partner," the myth of relationship being about changing someone, dealing with (and avoiding) conflict, communication, why you really have a problem when you think you have no problems, and how many people you've actually got in bed with you.

Enjoy the ride!

Chapter 6

Conflict: Avoiding It vs. Embracing It

Conflict: Avoiding It vs. Embracing It

So, let's start with acknowledging that your average bear (or bear-ette) really doesn't wake up each day thinking, "Who can I piss off today?" or "What conflict can I spend the day cultivating and duking it out with someone about?" If you're someone who actually *does* wake up like this, then this is the wrong book for you!

I believe that conflict, like anger, is not—in and of itself—a bad thing. What gets messy is when you don't know how to give it empowering meaning and how to masterfully "do" conflict so that you minimize damaging your relationship. Yet, so many people are *so* afraid of conflict (which is understandable, given how many of us have been deeply scarred by anger and angry actions) that they do *whatever* they can to avoid conflict, particularly in their love relationship. There are also others so scarred by emotional abuse in their childhoods that they actually become rage-a-holics that can't wait to get pissed off at someone. I want to be clear that this chapter is for those of you who are not rage-a-holics and who are clear you're fundamentally stable at your mental and emotional core. If you know or suspect you're not, you want to strongly consider getting psychotherapy and/or psychiatric help.

For us garden-variety neurotics, I'm inviting all of us to realize that *conscious* conflict is one of several ways to really enrich and enliven your relationship. Again, that's not to say I'm encouraging anyone to provoke conflict at every possible turn, but I am encouraging you to start shifting your mindset around conflict away from seeing it as proof of some serious problem and toward embracing it—when it organically occurs—as *proof* that your relationship still matters to you and that you're growing. The *damaging* kind of conflict is unconscious conflict, where you're proverbially shitting all over the relationship space because you're behaving unconsciously and are totally unconscious about what the conflict's *really* about. You're not considering how to resolve it in an enlightened, productive way as you would think to do if you were remembering that you agreed to a guiding principle of respecting your partner, and their divinity, no matter how challenging it may be at times.

Now, why am I being a cheerleader for embracing conflict? It's actually pretty simple. You, as a human being, are hardwired to connect, grow, and evolve. Relationships are a key vehicle for ensuring that all that happens—unless you're committed to trying to stay just one way for the rest of your life and you want your relationship to do the same (good luck with that, by the way). Add to that the fact that a lack of conflict in your relationship signals that you're stagnating and avoiding not only conflict but change. Consequently, you're not moving in the right direction. You're treading water, hoping you're not going to have to change and get uncomfortable.

There's a second reason people tend not to embrace conflict. Remember the chapter on ego relationship versus Spirit-led relationship in Section I? The shadow doesn't really like change, and it's willing to let us suffer interminably rather than have to feel the discomfort of change. Ironically, it can even use anger and rage as tools—as a deflection—for avoiding change.

I grew up with *that* model of relationship. My parents, who were married to each other twice with a ten-year intermission, both had their own terror around change, particularly my mom. She was afraid of so many things and had a PhD in worrying. She dealt with that by trying to keep as many things the same as she possibly could. My dad is a person who likes to shake things up to a fair degree (well, ok...he likes to shake things up most of the time), and he wanted to be out exploring people and life. This ended up being a constant source of conflict between them, where each of them found some false sense of power by seeing who could be more passive-aggressive or aggressively controlling with the other. When that didn't work, it became a contest to see who could out-yell and outlast the other.

On the surface, they looked like a couple that loved conflict; yet, the *source* of the conflicts rarely got resolved. Why? They rarely got handled because they couldn't see how strong the desire to avoid change was and they were unwilling or unable to truly acknowledge the numerous fundamental flaws in their relationship, because to do so seemed like it could only lead to them being on their own). So, they used unconscious conflict to keep them stuck and distracted from a lot of very uncomfortable and scary truths. [Moral #1: conflict without resolution and failing to do what you have to do to get to the true bottom of things get you nowhere.] Because they wouldn't get down to the nitty-gritty of the source of their conflicts, they ended up spending most of the last thirty-three years of their second marriage being *together*, for sure; but, they were pretty miserable for thirty-one of them, until the last year of my mother's life, when they seemed to realize that connection was far more important than "winning."

The most empowering role that conflict can play in a relationship is to keep the relationship—and each party in it—honest, on a growth edge from time to time (essential to long-term growth), and organically vibrant rather than stale. When you do conflict consciously and well, you push yourself and your relationship to never take anything for granted and to always be finding the edges of your comfort zone(s). Knowing where those edges lie enables you to challenge them so that you can open up so much in yourself that can pleasantly surprise you and your partner, in terms of the kinds of growth that you can have. If you build a relationship that embraces conscious conflict, you will have a filet kind of relationship, rather than a Gardenburger kind of relationship. It's like the difference between a diamond and cubic zirconium.

Let me show you what a conflict-avoidant relationship looks like and what it costs. When Helen and Steve came to me, they had been married thirty-four years—a second marriage for both. Helen was a very wise teacher and coach, empowering women in midlife to reinvent their lives by building their dream business. Steve was, essentially, retired. What drove Helen to reach out to me for help was the fact that she was realizing her anger toward Steve was growing and growing ... to the point where she was hard-pressed to be around him or to even want to talk with him. From her perspective, he was the problem. He was smoking too much, had gotten too fat (which was creating significant health challenges), and had little to no apparent interest in sex.

For her part, Helen had become a medium-grade workaholic trying to build her business, sublimating most of her time and energy into that, rather than the marriage (helped by a heaping pile of resignation she hadn't been honest with herself about). Helen's unhappiness had been building for *years*! This was not a sudden deterioration.

For Steve's part, he thought everything was okay. He knew Helen was irritated, but he chalked that up to some character flaw or issue in her that was her issue to deal with. He saw her as a nagging pain in the ass, rather than seeing how her "nagging" was the only way she figured she'd be able to get through to him since nothing else had worked. He hadn't noticed the correlation between him telling Helen he would do X and—because he rarely kept his promises—the escalation of her silent fuming and passive-aggressive way of ignoring him.

So, for quite some time, rather than really getting into it, having a conscious fight to clear some stale air, and really shifting things, they just believed their own BS that they were either okay or that there was no point to bringing anything up because it was just going to fall on deaf ears anyway ... so, just suck it up and take one for queen and country. Tragically, this is not at all an unusual situation. The good news (depending on how you look at it) is that your Spirit is not going to let you easily get away with putting your head in the sand—if for no other reason than you're hardwired to grow, and avoiding it for too long will always catch up to you in the form of pain that gets so bad you'll do almost anything to relieve it.

After building a container strong enough for transformation to happen in by helping them reconnect to the facts that they both missed each other (and the relationship they once had) and they wanted something better back, one of the first things I did with them was to have them start getting WAY more real with each other. I showed them how *not* allowing conflict was resulting in much more separation, resentment, hurt, disappointment, and loneliness. In other words, I first got them even more consciously connected to the cost of not bringing their conflicts to the surface, rather than leaving them where they had been hanging out ... in the underground, below the radar (or so they wanted to believe). After first gauging if they still had any love for each other left (which they did), I got them talking about what they wanted instead of what they were having. When they realized that, for all that seemed so different between them a lot of what they wanted was actually pretty similar, they had the hope and motivation to get after what the real problems were. Once they'd decided they wanted a new relationship with each other, they were primed for the fact that they were going to have to get to the bottom of how they'd gotten where they were so that they wouldn't repeat it.

With a *lot* of work—and getting uncomfortably more real with themselves and each other than they'd been in years—they are now a few years into a much happier relationship where they have learned to work with and embrace their differences (and conflict) while more successfully embracing and loving each other. They learned to see conflict as opportunity. They learned how to argue constructively and with compassion. They've started owning their own experiences: he's lost weight and stopped smoking, and she's backing off her business to a significant degree because she realized its lack of success had more to do with her not really wanting to be a full-time entrepreneur anymore.

From this story, there are some key points about conflict that I can offer and how to make it work better for you and your relationship:

- Boundaries – To use conflict well, you have to have clear, specific boundaries with yourself and your partner. You need to share them with each other. If you don't know what your boundaries are, then you start by sharing what you've seen never works for you when someone's communicating disagreements or challenges. You each have to continually hone what helps you feel safe to communicate, and you have to know that being willing to continually say things that may be challenging will also help you both trust each other more. Without trust, you won't get much value from disagreeing on things.

- Flexibility – You need to be very specific about the kinds of things that are negotiable and non-negotiable for you—life values, relationship values, and in communication approaches (see Chapter 10 for more on this). If you know what those are for each other, it makes it easier to more quickly discern whether you have a lot more negotiation to do, or if you can just simplify by cutting to the chase and agreeing to disagree on a given matter.

- Transparency – With 95 percent of the couples I've worked with, the biggest damage to the relationship is almost always from what *isn't* said, rather than what is. If you're in conflict and you want to try to resolve it, you *must* be honest with each other; otherwise, you're going to only make each other feel temporarily better instead of actually solve the problem. A short-term irritation is worth a long-term future that feels great to share with each other, so start with telling the authentic truth about what you think is the issue, and then be prepared to discover the issue is something completely different from what you thought.

- The Mirror – This is one of the most important points in this whole book. When you realize that most of the conflict you will ever encounter in your relationship is actually a conflict within and about *you*, it opens up new vistas for what's possible in your relationship. Unless your wife hits you with a pan or kicks you in the balls, most of what irritates you is about *you* being somehow out of alignment with yourself (more on that in the communication chapter coming up). You're mad that your woman isn't giving you enough attention? How much attention have *you* been giving *her*? You resent having to go to PTA meetings with her? Are you telling her why you resent it? Are you taking ownership for choices, or are you turning her into your mom? So before you really get into it with your partner (or even your kids), look in the mirror and see what you see when you know and own that you're *100 percent at cause* for your experience every minute of the day.

I'll close this chapter with a couple reminders. First, the idea is to get good, and then masterful, with managing conflict. Don't expect perfection. There will be times that you won't remember, or you'll be too hot. When that happens, one of you needs to call a time-out, go for a walk, and move your hot energy. Then, come back and revisit the conversation until you get complete with the issue at hand.

The second thing to remember, from the chapter in Section I on Spiritual relationship, is that if you're striving to live a Spirit-led relationship, even in conflict, your partner is your Beloved—Spirit in human form. So, don't talk with your partner in a way you'd never *think* of talking to the Divine consciousness itself.

Chapter 7

There's a Problem When It Looks Like There Aren't Any Problems

There's a Problem When It Looks Like There Aren't Any Problems

———————•◆•———————

One of the most oft-expressed statements I hear from men whose partners have almost literally *dragged* them in to see me is: "I didn't even realize there were problems," or a variation: "I knew we had some issues, but I didn't know things were *this* bad." Of course, this prompts the same question every time from me to them (and usually to the man first): "Why didn't you know things were this bad? Why are you so surprised with what your wife is telling you?" The most predictably common answer is, "Because we weren't fighting—my wife wasn't complaining or bitching at me … so I figured things were okay."

Answers like this reveal a list of breakdowns and problems that is quite long. For right now, however, let's say that the thing most clearly at or near the top of the list is that one or both partners are "checked out." They're in major denial, have perilously lowered standards, and are playing an undeclared game of chicken with their partner out of deep fear(s).

When I was still in the corporate world, I remember walking into the office of an engineer I respected and liked a lot who seemed uncharacteristically down or depressed. Jerry was normally pretty chipper and usually went out of his way to at least say "Hi" to everyone. I went into his office, closed the door, and asked him if he was okay. He told me he wasn't. He shared that the night before, his wife of thirty years (with whom he was still living, along with their teenage daughter) had served him with divorce papers. He was absolutely flabbergasted and crushed. He literally didn't see it coming ... even though most of their close friends did and wondered why it took his wife so long to do it.

Again, this is a tragically common situation that leaves lives, particularly children's lives, twisted all to hell as if they had been hit by a tornado, and it doesn't *have* to be that way.

In a relationship like the one above, there are some primary problems going on:

- You've both allowed things to get to the point where you've each unconsciously started defining "good" as "Things don't suck as bad as they could or often do." (As in, when Bob's asked, "How are things with you and Carol, Bob?" Bob says, "We're good!")

- There's a lot of confusion regarding the difference between contentment and complacency. Odds are that you've gotten so out of the habit of deep, conscious, and radically honest communication that complacency has come to feel like contentment ... and you've forgotten what actually makes you content.

- Your mind has convinced you that "silence is golden" because, if you stay silent, you won't hurt your partner in a potentially fatal (to the relationship) way. But, it's really about you being afraid of authentically dealing with what you don't even want to look at. So, you not only withhold all kinds of things from your partner, but you're pretty comfortable not asking him or her what's up with them and/or with settling for very surface answers.

Let's explore those problems in more detail, along with some things that you can do to prevent and/or rectify them.

Good Enough

Whether you're in the early stages of building a brand-new relationship for which you've designed the foundation—á la Section I of this book—or you've been in a relationship for some time, it's always critical to look at your standards for gauging whether you're happy, fulfilled, and in alignment with what your heart and Spirit really want and need. In the design phase of a relationship, you both should actually have your vision for the relationship, its broader purpose, and your key values for the relationship written out. For the building phase, you both should be brainstorming with each other on ways to measure how on track you are or aren't with what really keeps the relationship alive and evolving.

Things get to an "It's okay because it could be worse" place because you've either not gone deeply and clearly enough with yourselves and each other in the design phase—if you're in a newly unfolding partnership—or you've allowed any number of other things to become more important than your relationship. A great relationship sources everything; yet it becomes all too easy to unconsciously allow it to get relegated to second, third, or fourth place in your life. Part of why that happens is that some part of you gives up believing you can have what you want—often when you get triggered into old childhood stuff during an argument, for example—so you stop sharing and asking for what you desire and need. This often happens as a unilateral, solitary journey through the Hall of Mirrors in your mind, so you need to build ways, or systems, for doing the best you can to head things off at the pass before they calcify into stagnating, destructive patterns for the relationship.

This can include being sure you share with each other how you'll each be able to recognize that you're "hiding out," both individually and as a couple. Odds are that you both already know that, but it can be very powerful (and preventative) to name them out loud with each other. For example, you might hide behind literally saying "I'm fine" when you know perfectly well you're not. So you could tell your partner something along the lines of, "Well, you'll know I'm hiding out when I automatically tell you things are fine but my energy isn't matching 'I'm fine,' and when I go more than a day or two without really using more than a few syllables in any of my responses."

Now, it should be pointed out here that it is *not* your partner's job to "rescue" you or "draw you out." That's *your* job. However, what you *can* do for each other is to point out what you're aware of and invite each other to be more authentic. For example, "Honey, I know you're saying you're fine, but—to me—you seem pretty [fill in the blank with the energy you're experiencing in them ... like mad, sad, etc.]. Am I misperceiving that? If not, I'd love to hear what's really going on if you're willing to share it."

Another way to prevent things from just being "good enough" is to support each other in individual and collective pursuits that take you out of your respective comfort zones. If you're noticing that your social life (presuming you have one, which you need) has gotten into a rut or pattern of always being the same activities and the same people all the time, develop and share ideas with each other for new and different kinds of activities that you've either always wanted to do (or at least try out) but haven't allocated the time to. You want to try stuff that matters to your partner, even if it doesn't necessarily appeal to you, because it keeps the sense of being "for each other" strong, and it can open you to discovering that some old assumptions you've had about what you like or don't have changed without you even realizing it.

When my wife, Sarah, and I first started dating back in the early eighties, Sarah was not really into music. She liked what she liked whenever she was listening to the radio (which wasn't often), but music was neither a passion nor a hobby for her. However, for me, music is more than a passion—it's almost an obsession. Early on, I invited her to go to a Tom Petty concert with me. She didn't know Tom Petty from Richard Nixon, but because she wanted to experience what really lit me up, she agreed to go. She spent the whole evening standing on her chair at the amphitheater where we saw the show, dancing and whooping it up. This brought me huge joy, and we've gone to many, many concerts together since.

Similarly, she *loves* color, sewing, and design-related stuff, none of which interested me in the least. However, the first time she invited me to go with her to a fabric shop, I agreed to go because I wanted to learn more about what turned her on. I didn't come to fantasize about the next time we could go to a fabric store, but I quickly came to learn more about how colors and décor have to go together to create a mood and a vibe, particularly in our home. So, by learning more of her inner and outer world, I came to really appreciate and value all of what it takes to create a nurturing environment that people love to come into, for example.

Contentment vs. Complacency

Webster's defines *contentment* as "the state of being happy and satisfied; the state of being content." In my experience, people in general have very different criteria for what constitutes contentment for them. I would never presume to tell a person or a couple what is specifically required to guarantee contentment in or out of a relationship. Well, okay … I lied. I can think of one universal component of being content: being authentically aligned with who you really are, no matter what and no matter how long it takes you. However, that's tricky in or out of a relationship because a great number of people really believe they don't know who they really are. They don't understand that they actually probably *do* know who they are, but they've been trained not to let it out or show it. So a lot of us are walking around as we were trained to be rather than how we are authentically and uninhibitedly. However, if you go into building your relationship fully disclosing yourself, your desires, your perceived shortcomings, and your vulnerability, then the relationship has all the potential in the world to reveal to you what actually makes you content. Why? Because, more often than not, the *truth* brings and/or puts you into an eventual state of freedom that makes you friggin' happy! When you're being open and honest about where you are, deep connection with your partner becomes easier…not always *fun*…but easier.

Contentment is innately oriented around a moving target, which is to say that no one thing alone is likely to make you feel content. Contentment can be found in a series of innumerable moments with yourself, with nature, with your beloved, with your children, with a pet. The list of things that can engender contentment is endless. In a marriage, it isn't the structure of the committed relationship that creates contentment; it's simply an incredibly rich sandbox to play in to find your own inner contentment, moment to moment. You both can spur each other on for the entire life of the relationship to be seeking contentment and alignment, not just for your own pleasure but also because of what you can each generate in every area of your life from that place of being content.

Complacency, on the other hand, tends to be much more about stasis—staying put for the sake of predictability and "security." The Webster's definition of *complacency* is: "Self-satisfaction, especially when accompanied by unawareness of actual dangers or deficiencies." There's the rub. A *lot* of people really resist change because change is often *scary* to the shadow ego part of you. Consequently, while the heart orients toward contentment, the mind usually orients toward predictability, control, and minimization of distress or pain. So most of us are "doing" relationship to create a state of complacency (without even being conscious of it), within which anything that shakes things up is neither encouraged nor allowed.

When you're serving complacency, your dreams get narrower, what you'll tolerate will grow (as will all the bullshit you tell yourself to rationalize what's staying stuck and unrewarding), what you communicate will shrink, and your standards of excellence for the quality of your life and relationships will tank. You'll allow that for the sake of keeping yourself and your circumstances within your control (or so you'd like to think) and seemingly "safe." You'll be happy with things being the same, predictable way for a really long time. With complacency, your risk tolerance goes to hell in a hand basket, whereas contentment breeds a desire for more growth at some point.

The strongest construction for a relationship will come from the two of you:

- Discussing this topic for more than ten minutes early on in the formation of your relationship. Again, you want to lay out how you each define each of those two terms.

- Sharing the role both of those states played out in your previous relationships; particularly, how you show up (or not) when you're content versus how you show up when you're coasting or settling.

- Sharing times in your relationship history (and related to other parts of your life as well) when you felt content, and where and how you eventually drifted toward complacency. Follow that up by exploring which of your fears you were trying to protect, as it were, by hanging on to complacency. Also share how the complacency and contentment dynamics played out in your families of origin. While you're not doomed to repeat your parents' relationship, looking at how those energies impacted your family (and you) can be a reasonable predictor of what you can stumble into in *your* relationships.

- Creating a structure for checking in with yourselves—and each other—on a regular basis to keep cultivating contentment and warding off complacency.

Discomfort Is Actually Your Friend – If You Use It Well

A couple I work with, whom I'll call Bernice and Chet, are in their early forties with two young children. They have been together for twelve years. Bernice approached me because she felt that, after so many years together, there had to be more to marriage than she was experiencing. She was struggling with getting her business to really take off at the level she knew she was capable of. She knew that she had the skill and delivered a ton of value. Chet had been struggling to find his way professionally, not having ever found a career that really lit him up, which resulted in him having a series of unsatisfying, relatively low-paying jobs. This put a great deal of financial pressure on them, particularly with Bernice being a mom of two young kids *and* the main breadwinner—an entrepreneurial one at that. All of this stress was creating feelings of being overwhelmed and fatigued and a sense of always being in survival mode, and both of them were trying to figure out what was wrong and missing for them, individually, and as a couple. There was very little fun and very little sex. Each of them was just trying to do the best they could to eke out some kind of joyful experiences wherever they could (which wasn't much).

It didn't take long for me to discover how little they were sharing with each other. Both of them were doing what a great many couples seem to fall into doing, which is to live in their heads, trying to figure out what the hell's going on by themselves (doomed to fail, by the way, since you can't solve a problem using the same thinking/mindset that created it in the first place, as Einstein pointed out), suffering in virtual silence, and trying to figure out what the hell's wrong with their partner. For many, there's a misguided faith that if they could just figure out what's wrong with their partner, and then magnanimously point it out, their partner could just get their shit together, it'll all work out fine (see Chapter 11 for more details on why this can really never work). They were also hiding most of this and avoiding the feelings by pouring any little leftover free time into their kids, but not each other.

As I started digging more into why they weren't talking to each other, Chet said that he wasn't clear enough on what he even wanted, so what was the point of talking about it? It just seemed best to him to keep plugging away, trying to make the money he could, and enjoying what little time he had with the kids and the one recreational activity that he enjoyed when he could. Bernice was living in a steady state of resentment and confusion. She had little libido for Chet or anyone else and felt heartbroken that she couldn't have it all financially, professionally, and romantically. When I asked her why she wasn't communicating any of this to Chet—other than through passive-aggressive behaviors occasionally punctuated with outbursts of anger—she said she wasn't telling Chet much because she didn't want to make it worse by getting him even more upset. She didn't want to hurt his feelings; she felt certain she knew what he would say, think, and feel; and she also felt certain that it was screwed up and unfair to want what she really wanted, and she should just keep quiet while fantasizing about what a dream life could maybe look like in some lifetime. Their relationship was in real trouble and not getting better. Again, this is a depressingly common situation, even amongst people you think are highly aware and conscious, intelligent, and good communicators!

Hearing about all of this from each of them, together and separately, it became really clear that one of the key drivers behind the stuckness was that neither of them wanted to hurt the other, and neither wanted to feel their *own* pain, really. Ironically, of course, in the subconscious drive to not hurt or be discomforted, they were both in pain and very uncomfortable! Each of them, in their own way, related to both conflict and discomfort as "bad." They were each trying to figure out how to just get through it with as little additional suckage as possible, suffering in more silence (for the most part), with all of it based on assumptions of thoughts, feelings, and expectations they were sure the other one had.

The first order of business in working with them to start shifting this was to get them *talking* ... and talking *truthfully*, starting with what each of them was making up about the other's thoughts, feelings, and desires. Now, I'm not going to sugarcoat this. There *was* conflict and great discomfort. They spent many days and nights being pissed off, depressed, frustrated, and stubborn. But, because I wouldn't tolerate what they were tolerating with each other, I kept getting them to go more and more into what was scary and uncomfortable for them. Along the way, we've looked at how it wasn't their partner's job to change for them, but they each had a job to get clear about what they wanted, what was blocking them, and then how to work with all of that as a team. During the whole process, they came to see that, as long as they know how to communicate masterfully and responsibly, discomfort and emotional pain are actually allies for the well-being of their marriage. They serve as grist for the mill to keep their relationship growing, edgy (in a good way), and full of more fun because every time they've gone *into* the discomfort and pain, they've come out feeling so much better and more connected.

While the work with them continues, they are now having much more fun together, Bernice has quite happily reinvented her business in a way that's bringing her much more joy (and, thus, more energy), he's in the midst of dreaming again about what he wants to do for his career, and they are much more vulnerable with each other ... resulting in the two of them feeling more connected with each other than they've been in years.

In case it isn't clear from this example, trying to avoid discomfort, pain, and awkwardness creates *exactly* those things. If you're willing to allow discomfort and conflict to be your relationship's (and your) friend—because they show you that you still care about the relationship and have a commitment to it being vital and evolving for as long as you both shall live—you will have infinitely more inner freedom and more ease within the relationship. What you'll also have is a relationship built around faith in your own resiliency and in your own knowing, and in the bond between you being sufficiently solid enough to handle bumps in the road with each other. When you have all that, you have a relationship built around depth.

Anybody can just coexist together in a relationship—go to work, come home, take care of the kids, get laid once in a while—and wash, rinse, repeat until you croak. You're here for *so* much more than that, but it requires getting to know, love, and own your depth, and then being willing to allow your relationship to be one of the main vehicles for keeping that deliciously expanding. That requires each of you to relate to discomfort and even pain as essential ingredients that you don't avoid or run from anymore (not constantly—I'm not encouraging anyone to find their inner sadist and feel like shit every day) to having a luxury-home kind of relationship that will keep each of you growing and will grow with each of you. It also means that you don't conspire with your partner's subconscious mind and shadow by pretending not to see what's going on with them and keeping quiet about it. It's not your job to drag each other out of the caves we all go into from time to time; however, I'm strongly suggesting that it can be your contribution to your partner to shine a flashlight into that cave, let them know you know they're in there, and invite them to come out, trust you and each other, and start spilling the beans. It'll only hurt for a little while.

Chapter 8

How Many People Are Really In Bed With You Anyway?

How Many People Are Really In Bed With You Anyway?

———•◦•———

This book isn't a sex manual, contrary to what you may be thinking it means! There are so many variables and moving parts in a relationship, I don't believe it's possible to identify and keep track of every single one of them in every single moment. Life is too full, as it is, even if you could. However, when you're building a relationship meant to last, certain variables and issues are significantly common and pervasive enough they are worth putting at the top of your list of things to be aware of as much as possible. This chapter addresses one of the top three: there's way more than just the two of you in your bed (figuratively speaking) and running your relationship.

To help you start getting the picture, I have a few questions for you:

- If you have children, how often do you find yourself speaking with them and/or reacting to them the same way that one of your parents used to talk to you ... that you vowed, as a kid, you'd never do when you grew up?

- In the early stages of a new relationship, how often have you found yourself getting caught to some degree between your partner's wants and the wants of your parents/family of origin?

- Have you ever found yourself feeling very hurt by a comment that would normally never even faze you, but in a given moment, plunges you immediately into a rage or into feeling like you've suddenly shrunk to about an inch tall?

- Have you ever found yourself sulking because you didn't get something you wanted from your partner, even though you never told them you wanted it, and then gave them the cold shoulder for a day or two?

- Have you ever argued with your partner about money ... and then gone out immediately and spent money on something you really didn't need or that you knew would irritate the shit out of your partner?

These are all real examples that have come up either in me and/or in numerous clients over the years. They're examples of not being in your right mind—which actually isn't a bad way of looking at it. Oft times, you are not in *your* right mind. You (and every other human being) easily get triggered into going into a child's and/or teenager's mind; however, it's not just anyone's childhood or adolescent mind that you go into. It's *your* childhood or teenage mind you're actually in 95 percent of the time anyway; you just don't know it until something triggers you, like in the examples above. When that happens, you're not listening from your right mind (and heart) but from a web of emotional beliefs, traumas, and disappointments that immediately take you from the present and catapult you into the past. This includes taking you to past ways of trying to protect your heart from more pain and to gain a sense of feeling safe again.

In Chapter 3, in Section I of this book, I discussed the roles we bring to our relationships, along with the expectations we've taken on in our lives that just naturally migrate over to our relationships. As you and your partner are consciously working on and playing at building the strongest, most luxurious relationship on top of the foundation that you've designed for it, the rest of this chapter is going to highlight the key things you need to know, and to do, to help the most loving parts of your "inner family," as I call it, to support your relationship-building efforts. Let's start by defining what I mean by your "inner family."

Your Inner Family

The first thing to know about this topic is that you are not being singled out as one of the few f*d-up people that need to know this information. *Everyone* is dealing with what I'm saying here, one way or another. The only difference is in whether they're dealing with it consciously and proactively or not. As far back as the first third of the twentieth century, noted psychoanalyst Carl Jung was writing about the parts of our subconscious/unconscious mind that he labeled "subpersonalities." During World War II and shortly thereafter, British psychiatrist John Bowlby developed what came to be called "attachment theory," which describes how human beings respond within relationships when hurt, separated from loved ones, or perceiving a threat. Our ability to form secure, healthy attachments to others depends on our ability to develop basic trust in caregivers and self. Amongst the many who have written about attachment theory over the years, a key piece of it says, "An infant needs to develop a relationship with at least one primary caregiver for the child's successful social and emotional development, and in particular for learning how to effectively regulate their feelings." [Wikipedia excerpt on attachment theory]

In the sixties and seventies, developmental psychologist Mary Ainsworth found that:

> Children will have different patterns of attachment depending primarily on how they experienced their early caregiving environment. Early patterns of attachment, in turn, shape – but do not determine - the individual's expectations in later relationships. Four different attachment classifications have been identified in children: secure attachment, anxious-ambivalent attachment, anxious-avoidant attachment, and disorganized attachment. [also Wikipedia article on Attachment Theory]

Now, I have a habit of making things more complicated than they probably need to be. So rather than turn this book into a layman's psychology textbook, let me boil this down in a way that can easily answer a question that may be in your head by this point: "What in the hell is this dude talking about? Why the hell should I care, and what does this *really* have to do with relationships?"

There are a few reasons this is so important and why you should care:

- As I've discussed before, we are running around managing and doing our lives from our unconscious and subconscious "programming" about 95 percent of the time. The origin of that programming was largely from the third trimester of our gestation up until we were about seven years old. In case you're still not getting it, 95 percent of the time, you're handling things from the levels of thoughts, beliefs, experiences, and decisions of someone who is no older than seven. (If that isn't enough to give you pause for thought, I don't know what else is).

- Our first "classroom" for learning anything about relationships is our family ... especially our parents' way of doing relationship. (Does that already begin to start explaining a few things about what hasn't been working in your relationships so far?)

- Whatever your parents never got/have gotten handled and resolved in their relationship, you're subconsciously trying to handle it for them in *your* relationship.

- If you're a parent, your children's ages are going to bring up your unresolved, subconscious wounds and hurt from that same age.

Have I gotten your attention now?

All of us have these subconscious aspects or parts of ourselves that, in the eighties and nineties, were referred to as the "inner child." Because there are so many young parts of us, ranging from the "inner infant," if you will, up to the "inner teenager," I just find it easier to refer to all of these subconscious parts of us as the "inner family." In Section I, I shared the story of my wife, for example, asking me to empty the trash after I got done eating dinner, which precipitated a two- to three-day shit-fit on my part toward her, which I realized much later was a fifteen-year-old boy's energy inside me acting out ... when I was about thirty-two chronologically.

You'll never really know when these parts of you are going to get re-stimulated (thanks to our body's cellular memory of every damn thing that's ever happened to us, whether we remember it consciously or not) and suddenly take you over. When this happens, it's as if it came out of thin air, chloroformed you unconscious, stuffed you in the trunk of the car, and then started driving the car of your life—at age four, seven, eleven, or sixteen. If you want to ensure this happens frequently, get into a relationship (or become a parent). You can count on the fact that, until you *really* get to know those parts of you—how they "think," how they react, how they feel, and how they strategically tend to respond to perceived threats of danger and emotional pain—you're extremely susceptible to behaving in a way that disregards your relationship foundation and runs amok doing whatever is perceived to be needed to get safe and to avoid pain. If you're in the first year or two of being with a love partner (married or not), you can be assured that, when the hormones and infatuation with each other quiet down a bit, you're going to meet these parts, both yours and your partner's. Consequently, when you're beginning to build your dream relationship (and, really, over the life of it), you need to get intimately familiar with these young parts of yourself so that you can learn how to manage them, rather than the other way around, which is happening 95 percent of the time in your life right now.

Before sharing some ways to do this, it can't be overstated that these parts of you are *not* "the enemy." Attachment theory beautifully covers the patterns and defense structures that we had to develop when we were way too young to be able to take care of ourselves mentally, physically, and emotionally. When we were little, we needed these parts. Because we were so young and a bit helpless at the ages at which these all initially developed, we needed models. Unfortunately (or fortunately, depending on your circumstances then), the key models we all had to go by were our parents, grandparents, aunts, uncles, etc. We all pick up the best of our family of origin, but the worst also comes with the package. In other words, these young inner family parts of you and me ... they're not bad. They don't exist to make your life hell. They exist to try to protect you. They just don't realize that the ways they're trying to do it, and the reasons for activating their protective tricks of the trade aren't needed or age-appropriate anymore (i.e., how they were trained).

They were born out of actually experiencing trauma, hurt, dis-attachment (in the case of abandonment), being smothered or neglected, etc. So these parts of you are not the bad guys to be eliminated and swiped off the face of the Earth. They need to be loved into submission, as one of my early mentors used to say. How do you love them? You give them loving, compassionate attention while helping them see that there are alternatives to the ways they've been used to interacting with the world. In other words, show them more resourceful ways of being, protect them (as the adult that you are), and show them alternatives. They'll calm down and back off. It's kind of like Jessica Rabbit said in *Who Framed Roger Rabbit?*: "I'm not bad, I was just drawn that way!"

Identifying Key Players

Okay, each of you wants to get familiar with the most prevalent of these inner kids, or inner family parts. A good starting point is to look at your primary caretakers when you were growing up. All of us have some version of being a kid and saying, "I'll never be like *that* when I grow up." Yet, predictably, we all have aspects of our parents that we act out without even thinking about it. It was both humbling and very relieving to discover that my old way of dealing with hurt feelings of passive-aggressively killing off people with silence, killer looks, and abject inattention wasn't really me. I grew up watching my mom behave like that whenever her depression or rage got out of hand and I was on the wrong end of it. She was my model.

As I spent seventeen years leading workshops oriented toward healing the inner family, I learned that different ages come up at different times, but there are some of these parts that tend to be the most prevalent—the ones that believe they're best equipped to keep the most urgent and scary threats at bay. You could call these the "front-line bodyguards." When you were a kid and discovered how to keep people from getting too close or hurting you too much, that same method is going to show up today as one of those front-line bodyguards.

To give an example, as a really young boy (before I started going to school), I was very outgoing, liked a lot of affection, and was very playful. However, when I started nursery school (yep, that's what it was called back then in the early sixties), because I had a cleft palate, harelip, and a speech impediment resulting from those, it didn't take long for kids to start making fun of me for how I looked and how I spoke. It would either take the form of outright ridicule or exclusion, both of which were extremely painful and frustrating. I didn't understand why I was being treated that way because I thought I was a good person and didn't see anything I was doing as wrong or bad. Eventually, it got painful enough that I needed a way to protect against and buffer the pain of going to an environment every day that just felt bad. So I suppressed my natural exuberance and desire to play with others and became a loner. I was five when this part of me was born. The truth was I wanted connection more than anything in the world, but it was "safer" and less painful to pretend that I didn't need or want it. That "loner" became what I've referred to above as a "part" ... my "loner part." (It's useful to give our parts a name.) As I got older and had to start standing in front of a class and speaking, where I could get teased by a larger group than just a few bullies, I got terrified to get up and talk. So my loner part began to come up with ways to dodge having to get up in front of the class. (You can imagine what that part of me is going through writing a book, even at fifty-seven!) I built an image of someone that was aloof, stuck-up (that's what others thought, even though I was anything but), and didn't need anyone else. Everyone became a default threat, and people had to somehow prove to me that they were "safe" and truly wanted to know me and be a friend.

As I got older, that evolved into a persona that seemed detached and didn't really need people. This morphed into a "shy" part. For most of my life, I identified myself as a shy person, not knowing I was actually experiencing a shy *part*. The truth about me is that I *love* people and thrive on connection. But that part got forgotten and buried under the parts that felt their job was to keep me from hurting any more than I already did. I *really* believed I was inherently shy. Not knowing it was a childhood part of me running the show, conversations with people could be excruciating. The only conversations that weren't painful were the ones I had with certain adults that saw through it and helped bring out more of the "natural" me. This is part of what motivates all of us to get into relationship, by the way. We all want to be seen and loved just for who we are. If we've experienced that as a rare thing and get terrified of trusting it when it does show up, then someone who can pierce that inner-family shield and hit our heart will often be someone we start loving— we just don't always know that it's a child inside us that's falling in love with the surrogate mom or dad that our prospective mate seems to be.

Because we can't ever really know our prospective partner's parts up front, and vice-versa, what's going to happen—no matter how well you've designed the foundation for the relationship—is that initial period of infatuation, lust, and constant wanting to be together is going to dissipate and fade. When it does, then the strongest childhood wounds that stem from childhood things like emotional neglect, smothering, abandonment, emotional abuse, sexual abuse, betrayal history, and others are going to start coming up as the attachment issues get more visible because the idealized infatuation phase is no longer the dominant energy in the relationship. Then, depending on whether your inner children have decided to hide/withdraw (like mine did) or get what they need by developing an aggressive and/or clingy strategy, those front-line parts are going to start emerging in ways that are likely to be embarrassing at best, and horrifying at worst. In the spirit of the best defense being a strong offense, then one of the key things that will help you build the strongest relationship is to begin with identifying your key inner players first.

There are a couple ways to do this. The first is to take an inventory of your top three to five emotional wounds in a manner that's as brutally honest as you can muster. (And if you can't, I strongly recommend finding a therapist or coach skillful at fleshing these kinds of wounds out and helping you heal them and their control of your life.) An unwillingness to do this, no matter how scary it is, only ensures these wounds will run you and your relationship more often than not, which is *not* good! To give you a sample list to get started, these could be wounds like:

- Nobody wants me or would love me if they knew who I really was and what I was *really* like. (an emotionally neglected wound)

- Don't leave me! (an abandonment wound)

- I'll take care of you no matter what, and don't worry about my own needs. (a different shade of an abandonment wound that hopes to be wanted by being a seemingly indispensable partner)

- The only way I can really be loved is to do everything for my partner that I can possibly do, prove I'm superhuman, and, thus, worthy of their love. (a wound that stemmed from getting love and attention for what you did as a kid, rather than for who you were)

- I'm not getting what I need from my partner, but I'm getting something, so I should just be thankful for what I am getting—and shame on me for wanting more. (a wound that often comes from being treated as a surrogate spouse by a parent and having affection withdrawn when the child wants to begin asserting their sovereignty and desires)

- I have no voice and no real power. (a result of being either drowned out by others in the family or blatantly told to be quiet/belittled for what you would say)

Once you've identified them, you want to then take your own assessment of how these have shown up in your life (particularly in relationships of all kinds, but especially romantic ones). Then, go to your closest friends—and any former lovers with whom you may still be on good terms—and ask them to share with you if they've ever noticed what you've noticed from doing the assessment. Ask them to give you specific observations and reflections of when they've seen any signs of any of these wounds and defense patterns (not to mention ways they may have noticed that you cover up the wounds—like being a perfectionist, for example). Be sure to reassure them that you're asking for this feedback penalty-free. They have to be assured that you're not going to rip their head off for telling the truth. It's also important to tell them *why* you're asking.

Ideally, your partner or prospective partner will do the same. If so, then you want to share with each other what you've found out. It'll likely feel risky, scary, and highly vulnerable. However, if you're not willing to go to any of those three places with yourself and your partner, your relationship already has a potentially fatal weakness in the foundation that will make anything you build on top of it unstable and vulnerable in a way that you won't like.

The second way to identify the key influential parts in your inner family is to take a cold, hard, and un-whitewashed view of your family of origin. Recent research indicates that 50 percent of our happiness has everything to do with genetics. We already know that emotional patterns can be genetically transmitted down through generations. While you may not have ever known your great-great-grandmother, the way she handled emotions and situations could very well be playing a role in how *you* do! The quickest way to identify who your inner kids tend to emulate the most is to look at which people in your family most hurt and irritated you as you were growing up … and how they did it. Then you want to look at where you have been doing the same thing to others (partners, lovers, kids, friends, co-workers, for example) as an adult. You can also look at how hard you work to be totally different from that person or those people, by the way. Whether you're trying to be like someone you admire, or you're working hard to be the *anti*-someone who hurt you deeply growing up, you're not being *you*. Since one purpose of a dream relationship is to support each other in being the best version of the real you that you dare to be, you want to know how you and your partner unconsciously and repetitively behave like who you're not. So, kinda like a CSI investigation, you and your sweetie want to really look at where you're already replicating patterns that you'd rather not share with each other.

It's also helpful to remember (don't worry … I know I'm repeating myself) that very few people will bring these young, wounded parts up faster than a lover/partner or one of your children. If you have kids, at whatever age they are at any given time, they're going to trigger your wounds from that same age (along with all your cool, fun, magical sides of yourself at that age, by the way). Your partner is likely going to trigger stuff you have with a parent. At this juncture in my life, I've come to see that there's a fair amount of truth to the old cliché that men marry their mothers and women marry their fathers. More to the point, we tend to unconsciously (for the most part) be attracted to qualities in someone that seem like the idealized parent that we really didn't have enough of (if at all) and that our inner kids are still looking to find. Once you're able to remove those idealized projections, things usually get easier and more fun.

So, all this may seem like it's bordering on "out there," talking about these "inner kids" and shit. However, if you do what I suggest above—and do it rigorously—you'll see that this whole subject is quite real and that it's mission critical for building a relationship that will last in a truly fulfilling way.

Starting to Get More Room in the Bed

Once you've identified the key inner parts that are already causing some disconnection and mischief, then you can start using a few tools to be able to begin getting the extra people out of your proverbial bed (though I could write a whole chapter on how this gets into one's sex life with a partner). You not only can thin the ranks that are crowding the connubial chamber, but you can also get yourself on the right track to start healing those parts of you that, really, don't want to keep feeling so scared, angry, hurt, and immobilized/immobilizing.

I've used a few *key* tools and techniques with people over the years that I was taught by one of my favorite mentors, Denny Gregg, who trained me in leading Inner Child Workshops back in the early nineties, and they're just as effective now as they were then.

All of these are predicated, by the way, on the assumption that you've got a basic handle on the most prominent (which is to say the most *active*) of these internal parts and that you're committed to working with them in a way that helps them heal and allows your adult resourcefulness to be more at the forefront of your relationship.

The first crucial step is to know when you have, in fact, been triggered and have "gone young." In other words, you need to practice and get masterful at distinguishing between whether you're operating from your adult self or from some part of your inner family. There's one really easy tool for doing that: **Remember that any upset or distress you have that lasts more than half an hour isn't about *now*.**

Think about it. If something happens that pisses you off, you usually can communicate quickly, get stuff off your chest, and then move on. However, if you find yourself getting mad or hurt by something that someone says (or doesn't say, which I find more prominent in relationship), and you essentially shut down and shut that person out for the rest of the day or week, you are not in your adult or even in present time. You've gone young, and you now have the challenge of getting back to the present and to your adult wisdom and skills at working through stuff. What comes part and parcel with this is an inability to stop obsessing on whatever got you upset, along with really strong feelings that don't dissipate for a while.

You can also consider how you're communicating (or, more likely, how you're *not* communicating). If you get upset and you can't even talk, or if you find yourself wanting to rip the other person a new one, using language and being in an energy that's disproportionate to the "offense," you've gone young. For example, every time a former client of mine made a mistake, they would unleash on themselves the cruelest, nastiest, profanity- and judgment-laden tirades. That was a habit of their dad's. The dad would do it to himself, the hired help, and to my former client as a young kid and teenager, so they'd do it to themselves, their kids, and their ex-spouse.

Once you've figured out you've been triggered and gone young, your first priority is to try to calm that young part down ... in a loving, compassionate way. No human being likes to feel ignored, marginalized, and/or attacked. We all want to be heard, at the very least. So that young part of you that's gotten triggered and is now running the show in a given moment wants the same thing. They need to be heard, they need to be felt, and then they may need helping getting the distressed energy released—what my first mentor refers to as "moving energy."

Energy gets stuck in our bodies and needs to be moved. To give you an example, my client John had a situation at work recently that got him really upset. He couldn't stop thinking about it for days and got himself into a tizzy of worry, anger, and righteous indignation about being asked to take on some responsibilities that he felt were beneath his pay grade, so to speak. He was about to have a meeting with his new supervisor and was all *verklempt* about it. After asking him a few questions, I got the sense that a big part of this upset had to do with a previous incident at work that I guessed he'd never really been able to vent about and come to peace with, and this current situation was bringing *that* stuff back up and causing a lot of old shit to get piled onto this situation. We pinpointed what was similar, I asked him if he was still pissed off about this earlier incident, and he felt into himself for a minute and said, "Yep!"

I taught him a simplified version of Hal and Sidra Stone's voice-dialogue process they pioneered in 1972. I had John set up two chairs across from each other and told him to identify which person/people he was most mad at and hurt by from the earlier incident. Then I told him to sit in a chair, imagining himself to be that person delivering the news to the "invisible" John in the other chair and to say it out loud just like it had happened in the earlier situation. Then I told him to move to the other chair, being John at that time, and to say *everything* that he'd wanted to say at the time it originally happened, in the authentic voice, tone, and language that he would have liked to have used back then, had it not been with a boss at the time ... and had John not had a boy inside who was raised to keep quiet and who was taught his voice and wants weren't important. I told him, "Just rip that person a new a*hole—no holds barred."

John did as I coached him to do, moved a ton of old, stuck anger, hurt, and resentment toward his old boss, and went into the meeting with his new boss feeling more spacious inside, open-minded, and ready to deal with whatever the new boss had to say with grace and ease. In that meeting, by the way, John found out just how much shit he'd been making up in his head about what he was going to hear, and he felt empowered and good about how the meeting turned out. This was also helped by the fact that the new boss got to deal with the adult version of John, and not the eight-year-old John that was ready to kick ass and take names after years of having his voice, needs, and truth shut down and marginalized.

Another technique for being able to both get what's really going on with that inner part and to start calming it down pretty quickly is what I (and my teachers) call "the two-handed writing technique." Here's how it goes: Let's say you go to bed one night in a perfectly great mood. You get into bed feeling great (and maybe even a little frisky). Your partner, however, barely gives you the time of day when you get into bed (and sure as hell isn't going to give you anything more than that), yet you don't let it really get to you. You kiss your partner goodnight, and you have a great night's sleep, far as you know. However, when you get up, you feel sad, a bit pissed, and just generally low energy, not wanting to really talk with anyone. In other words, you wake up feeling very different from how you felt when you went to bed the night before!

So, because you've read this book, you find a private space in the house or outside, and you take a pad and pen with you. On a piece of paper, you write the following words: "Good morning Geoff! (I'll use myself as an example). I'm noticing you feel pretty upset—sad and angry. Is that true? If so, would you be willing to share what happened?" As soon as you write that sentence, you put the pen in your other, nondominant hand and just start writing or even doodling. The words will begin to come as long as you don't try to first think what the answer is in your head and then just copy it all down. The trick is to imagine yourself being a conduit for that subconscious part of yourself to speak through, using your nondominant hand.

The upset kid may "say" something like, "Well, all I wanted to do was get a hug from [spouse] and she was so mean to me. It just really made me mad and hurt my feelings." Right there, you've found out that that part of you got triggered into an old wound of being ignored and/or rejected a few too many times as a kid. So you could write, "What did that remind you of? When did that happen before?" You put the pen in your other hand and just start writing whatever comes. You can then let that part of you know, through your dominant hand, that you can feel that upset, that you remember now what that was like, and tell them that the good news is that you're both in the present, that that circumstance that got re-stimulated will never be able to happen again, and that you—the adult—are there now to protect the young parts *and* the adult parts.

It took me more time to write this than it takes to use that tool. What's important is that you be consistent in using it. It can take anywhere from ten to thirty minutes to do, but it's one of the wisest time investments you can possibly make. If you both take the time to check-in with your inner family each morning before going to work (I do it after meditating), it would be a matter of writing, "Good morning, _____. How are you today?" Then, switch hands and see what they have to say. Doing that as a pretty regular, if not daily, practice will help those young parts calm down and feel safe and loved, and it will result in being triggered less often while being able to get "unhooked" much more quickly.

One other thing that may help make this tool even more effective is if you have pictures of yourself as a child that really touch your heart when you look at them. If you look at those before you sit down to do the writing, it begins to help you connect with that part of yourself energetically. You could also close your eyes and imagine yourself at that age, letting an image spontaneously come into your mind's eye. Then you can visualize yourself as you are today, coming into that image in your imagination, letting that adult image interact with the young one. The feelings can be quite sweet and heart-opening. I often encourage couples to create an altar in their room that not only contains pictures/images and sacred objects that remind them of whatever divine energy or consciousness they believe in, but that also has pictures of each of them as kids so that it's harder to forget that you each have that inner family that needs and wants a little loving each day to keep the misery away.

Lastly, for those who are particularly good at visualization and don't feel drawn to the two-handed writing technique, I'll give you one other exercise you can do to help get free of an inner-child reaction and get back to letting your adult self handle conflicts in a much better way. When you realize that you've gone young (don't forget the thirty-minute rule I gave you above), just do the following exercise that can take five to ten minutes to do at the most.

1. When you notice that you are in the middle of an upset that is making you "present" to your inner child's pain, find a quiet place to be still and be with that "little you." If you can't do this in the middle of your workday, just go into a restroom for a moment and tell them that you understand they are upset. Make an agreement with them that you will get back with them as soon as you get home. THEN KEEP YOUR PROMISE!

2. Once you are still, close your eyes, put your hand on your chest (your heart spot), and see how old you are in the upset by saying, "I feel like I'm ____ years old." Then see yourself at that age in your imagination, and just let them show up.

3. Leave your hand on your heart and say, "I feel just like when _____," and let an incident show up. Usually, it happens effortlessly.

> Like this: "I feel stupid, just like when the people in my seventh-grade class made fun of me in science."

Then just allow yourself to feel the pain with them so that they are not stuck with that stuff anymore. Press your way through the pain—even if you feel you can't because it hurts too much—until it subsides and you quiet down.

4. The primary thing to remember is that your inner child is just saying, "Hey! I'm in some pain here. Can you help me get rid of it by feeling it with me so that I don't have to carry it around anymore?" Once they feel their pain has been "gotten," it dissipates rather quickly!

5. Remember too that if you need help through this process, call someone—a good, trusted friend/family member or your coach if you have one—and tell them you just need someone to be with you while you feel your way through it. Ask them to support you in continuing to embrace it. NOTE: For friends who are not used to supporting you this way, there may be some discomfort around this request. It may bring up their need to protect you so that you won't trigger *their* pain. It is important to "shop at the right store" and know who is appropriate to call upon for support.

As I wrote about in Chapter 3 regarding roles, expectations, and assumptions and how influential they are in your relationship, it's wise to remember that a lot of those were all formulated in your childhood. So they *will* show up in your relationship—frequently. Developing this ability to connect with those younger parts of yourself (including your adolescent parts) and to support your partner when they've gotten hooked can save you a great deal of unnecessary pain, struggle, and destructive damage.

To support your partner, I often recommend both partners develop a verbal and nonverbal signal to give each other when they can see that their partner's been triggered. You want a signal or code that lets that triggered person have a chance to recognize they're hooked and, in doing so, be able to use any of the tools I've included here to get back to present time. I have one couple that uses hand signals. Another good one can be to make eye contact, be sure you're in a truly compassionate place, and say, "How old are you feeling right now?"

In closing this chapter, I just want to say that many people grew up having no voice, or feeling like they didn't, within their families growing up. Consequently, when they get strongly emotionally triggered, they tend to clam up. If you're at all competent with feeling your partner's energy, this "contracting" will be noticeable in both their facial expressions and energy. When this is going on, the most helpful thing you can do—even if it means you have to temporarily suck up your own upset—is to soften your energy and your tone of voice. Why? Because even though the *body* you're dealing with is adult, inside, in that moment, your partner's feeling like a kid and not likely all that able to tell the difference in that moment. So softening your tone of voice, like you hopefully would if you were dealing with a real, physically young child when they're scared shitless or in deep pain, will help your partner's inner child calm down enough to be able to bring some adult resourcefulness back into the picture. Once you can begin calming down the young part(s), the grown-up communication that it takes to work through your relationship challenges is more likely to be successful. (See Chapter 10 for suggestions on how to communicate effectively.)

Chapter 9

Living with the Invisible Partner

Living with the Invisible Partner

You may be wondering what the hell I mean by an "invisible partner." Well, let me tell you the story of a couple that will perfectly illustrate what I mean.

Jason and Pamela are both in their early thirties, highly educated, white-collar professionals, and in their first marriage (and, really, in their first "serious" relationship with anyone). They've been together for ten years and have a child under five years old. Jason works for a company that requires a commute of nearly three hours a day, so he leaves for work at seven thirty in the morning and usually gets home around seven at night. Pamela works from home as an entrepreneur. When they sit down to dinner, Pamela experiences Jason as someone who talks very little, doesn't seem like he's really listening (checking his phone while she's speaking, is pretty much a dead giveaway), and he doesn't seem to emotionally engage much with their child. On weekends, Jason spends at least eight to ten hours per day on Saturdays playing video games with friends, often at his and Pamela's home. While he does that, Pamela spends most of the time entertaining and supervising their child. For quite a while, their sex life has been virtually up to Pamela to create, run, and manage. She's tried talking to Jason to tell him how this feels, and his usual response is to either change the subject or to leave the room and hope that it will all go away. When he *does* address Pamela's concerns, he makes promises he doesn't keep. He also tells her that he thinks things are fine with the two of them, doesn't understand why she's getting upset, and doesn't want anything more than what they've got. He tells her he doesn't understand why she's so upset so often. Needless to say (though I'm going to say it anyway), Pamela has built up what has felt like an insurmountable wall of resentment, focuses on her work and being the best mom she can be, and gets most of her social intercourse from girlfriends who keep asking her, "WTF are you doing in this relationship?!"

Getting the picture? Pamela's living with a man who, when he's physically home, is essentially invisible—not present, not engaged, often unresponsive—appearing to live his life as an ostrich. Now, because it takes two to make or break any adult relationship, Pamela definitely has her role in this. Her anger has come out blatantly and sideways with stinging comments, if not outright yelling, at Jason. When she does that, it undoubtedly sends his inner kids back to the pain and difficulty of dealing with remote and absent parents who didn't teach him how to communicate or how to be heard. His way of seemingly blowing her off and leaving *her* feeling invisible and uncared about definitely reminds her of her father that she adored growing up, but who was absent most of the time and didn't get her when he *was* with her. She pursues and he runs. In many relationships, this will happen in one form or another. Two people with adult and childish wants and needs try to get them met one way or the other, but each is at a loss as to what they can do.

In one form or another, this is a very common underlying dynamic that underscores how important it is to be a *visible*, *present* partner. You wouldn't have only one person build your actual house, would you? One person can't be singlehandedly responsible and accountable for keeping a relationship vibrantly thriving. Both parties have to be committed to the health of a relationship no matter what, and that requires being as present as you can possibly be. That's what this chapter is all about: Presence.

What *is* Presence?

In my experience, there's no single, definitive definition of *presence*. If anything, it's kind of like the Supreme Court's take on obscenity back in the sixties, where the Court said, essentially, "We can't define it, but we know it when we see it!" In today's frenetic, nonstop way of living life, it's probably more common to be able to sense when someone's checked out (that would be the opposite of "being present," just so we're using well-defined terms, along with "living in your head"). Because this book is intended to be primarily for men (and also helpful to women), I'm going to use a definition of *presence* that was given in a seminar by my friend Joanna Kennedy, who was teaching how to heat things up between lovers. She defined *presence* in regards to men as the way it feels when a man enters a room *so* present that he energetically shows up as a "walking energetic erection." It's not about literally having an erection, but showing up as the energetic equivalent of a healthy, strong erection. When Joanna said that, every man and woman knew exactly what she was talking about, given how the men were laughing and most of the women were nodding their heads, going "Um-hmmm!"

A man in that kind of energy is in his body, is aware of the energy in the room, is comfortable in his own skin (in every way), is able to make eye contact with anyone and seem like he sees right into you, is aware of the energetics of the whole room, feels each person in the room, and communicates in such a way as to make it clear that—if he's listening to you—he hears every word you're saying ... as well as what you're *not* saying out loud. His intuition is strong and awake. With that energetic erection quality, he's not necessarily dominating, but he's clearly in charge of himself enough to relax anyone else that's around him because they just *feel* that he's got his shit together (how's that for a definition?) in the moment. When you're fully present, your partner's mind can usually relax somewhat because it won't have to worry as much about whether they're being fully heard or not. Someone who's really present when someone's talking will be able to reflect back everything they've heard in a way that the other party doesn't have to question if they were fully heard and understood.

What Presence Isn't

When someone asks, "Are you hearing me, honey (or Dad or Mom)?" it boggles my mind (and, in full disclosure, I've done it) how anyone can honestly feel any kind of integrity when they say, "I sure am, dear," while they're checking their text messages while their partner or kid is talking to them. Presence is a state of *being* that's acutely tuned in to everything going on in a 360-degree arc. If you think you're able to multitask with your attention, you're full of shit. Presence is not hearing every other word, nodding your head, and pretending to actually understand what's being said—and *why* it's being said. You're not really present if you're not listening to both what your partner is saying verbally and what's being said *energetically*. What do I mean by that?

How many times have you gone into a big party, a business meeting, or a bar and, within minutes, sized up who you want to connect with and who you want to stay the hell away from before anyone really says a word to you? We all have had some experiences like that. What makes that possible is the way our body is able to viscerally feel and read energy, give our brain input about said energy, and then allow our mind to figure out what to say and/or do with the energy being tuned into. When you're in a club and walk by someone who strikes you as pretty hot, it often isn't simply a matter of them looking hot. You eavesdrop on them, or just hang out near them for a while, and you can feel their sensual and sexual energy that turns you on. We *feel* pheromones—they don't talk out loud to us. So we all have the capacity to feel the energy of a person and of a room. To do that, however, requires us to be present ... and present in the present moment.

Presence is *not* listening to your partner and picking up just enough of what's being said to start formulating your response, your strategy for dealing with the issue being discussed, at least two plans for responding based on how you're sure the other person's going to respond to something, and then two contingency plans for what you'll do if it all goes to shit ... all while you're looking them in the eye while they're talking to you! Being present is *not* interrupting someone while they're talking to present one of those premeditated responses, thus helping them realize that you really haven't heard all of what they're saying, which often has adult and inner kid parts alike all start feeling like you don't really care what they're saying. This doesn't bode well for being connected or intimate with someone.

Being present is *not* initiating a conversation with your partner while you're shaving, brushing your teeth, watching Dr. Phil (or NASCAR), or taking a leak. If you are not making and maintaining eye contact, consciously breathing while you're listening, telling your mind to hush up when it wants to try to remember your shopping list while your partner's talking to you, and sitting or standing close enough to your partner without any other object in your hands being fiddled with, you're not present.

Now, if you're pretty present and your partner says something that triggers a wounded reaction, you're not going to be present to them or the conversation once that happens (see Chapter 6 for what to do when that happens). Once you get back to yourself, you also won't be present—yet—when you're hearing them but thinking about the last time they pissed you off or what you're going to do tomorrow to make it up to them, etc. You cannot be present unless you're in the present moment— not the past or the future, neither of which actually exist anyway, in each moment.

You also know you're not really present when you're unable to reflect back to the other person what they just said to you or if you're only focusing on the feelings being stirred up, making it near impossible to be truly feeling the other person anymore.

<u>Consistency Is Key</u>

Let me just cut to the chase. Being present only occasionally (like when your partner's telling you in no uncertain terms that you're checked out and would you kindly get the fuck back to listening to them) will never cut it. Consistency is key. I've lost count of how many men I've worked with—with their partners or individually— that have made innumerable excuses for being checked out by saying something along the lines of, "I just don't understand what her problem is! I'm listening to her, dammit!!" When I ask, "Okay ... did you do what she asked of you or make sure that she knew she was heard?" they frequently say, "Well ... no, I guess not. I nodded and told her I understood. Then, I just forgot to do what she asked me to do."

No one is perfect. Being fully present 100 percent of the time is not an achievable goal, in my opinion. However, if I had to give a rough percentage of how often guys that I've worked with are present in regards to their relationships, I'd have to say the average is about 50 to 60 percent. While better than a sharp stick in the eye, it's still not enough for a partner to be able to really feel safe enough to be fully vulnerable and authentic with you. It also won't help them feel safe to bring up stuff that they're upset about, stuff that's *really* important to them, that they know is likely to be really challenging to hear and talk about. If they have to worry about you blowing a gasket *and* not being present and accountable, they're likely to do the old eggshell walk and not really communicate. Then the issue(s) will rot like garbage in a landfill underneath the foundation of your relationship.

Your relationship is dead in the water if you two don't have and expand upon deep trust in each other. A lot of men have said they believe that they're trustworthy because they don't lie to their partner and they make promises. Yet between lies of omission and all the times they say they'll do something and then don't, they're lying way more than they think. Words are cheap, and I can tell you that women, in particular, don't trust what a man *says* as much as what he *does*. One of the key ways both of you will be able to build rock-solid trust is to be consistently present with your partner when you're with them (and listening to them) and doing what you say you're going to do. The more you don't do that, the more you make *yourself* invisible and—by extension—your partner and their needs/wants invisible. It's not all about that bass … it's all about that consistency.

Before giving you a few exercises you can do to help yourself be more present more of the time, I want to be sure to mention something about being with a partner who feels invisible to you more often than not. Before you try to get them to be different, it's a good idea to take a look at what their behavior (or lack thereof) is mirroring to you about yourself. Most of the time when we're upset with someone, it's got a lot to do with what they're energetically replicating (unknowingly, most of the time) from our past (and *who* they're replicating from our past). In other words, if you're frustrated that your wife isn't talking with you as much as you want, especially when you can just feel there's something up with her, take a look—before you come down on her in any way (or passive-aggressively just check out)—at where you do the same thing. Look at how much you're communicating something that's really troubling you, or are you simply resorting to one of the male go-to's: "I'm fine!"? Look at and take the risk of sharing your fears regarding opening up to your partner and being authentically vulnerable with them. Once you've got that nailed down, when you do try to talk with your partner about their (in)visibility, you won't be as likely to project your fears and self-judgments on them. Getting more proactively vulnerable and communicative yourself will help your partner do the same, more often than not.

Secondly—speaking to women in particular—is to try to avoid nagging a man into visibility, since it generally amplifies the problem. On the other hand, if nothing else has worked, it's probably a strategy of last resort.

However, you need to remember that there's a high likelihood that, on an unconscious level, your man's mother issues are getting projected onto you anyway. So if you nag or aggressively chase and/or shame a man to start opening up, you're likely to throw him right back into his childhood stuff, and he'll either clam up and/or run. The old saying, "You get more with sugar than vinegar" is true, more often than not. It isn't about needing to cover anything up or window-dress something. It's just about what kind of energy you're in at a given moment. If you're replicating an in-law that you already know your partner has issues with, you're not going to be heard or gotten. Making a request is one thing; nagging or demeaning him is another. If you take a chance and share your heart as you make a request, you're more likely to get a much better response. It also can help to softly touch him on his arm, shoulder, or hand, if it seems safe to you to do so. That gentle touch can help him get back in his body and be present.

In Section III, I'll share more about when a chronic level of invisibility and being checked out is cause for seriously looking at whether you're in the right relationship or not. For now, I'll just offer the advice to try sugar first when trying to ignite more presence with and from your partner. Now, let's look at a few things you can do to start increasing your level of presence, both on your own and with your partner.

<u>Ways to Get Present</u>

While there are *many* different ways to get more present in the moment, I'm going to share only the Top 5 on my Hit Parade. I particularly recommend partners practice these both on their own and together, as a regular routine of inner calisthenics:

- <u>Breathe</u> – This can't be overstated. Breathing is one of the best and quickest ways to get more present anytime and anywhere. If you notice you're getting irritated with your partner or child, for example, stopping dead in your tracks and spending three to four minutes simply closing your eyes (not while driving, of course) and taking the slowest possible deep breaths in and out will get you in your body and help calm down the parts of your nervous system that have been activated by whatever's gotten you all worked up.

- <u>Do a "Be-With"</u> – Simply put, a "be-with" is where you make eye contact, with your heart as open as possible (compassion will do as an acceptable substitute), for a couple minutes while also working on matching their breathing so that you're both literally breathing together. This is a good way to get present when you're not upset or in distress. I recommend this exercise within five minutes of getting home from work or before sitting down to eat dinner together, once you've either made a request to do so or have already adopted it as a daily practice to begin getting out of work head space and back to lover heart space. Ideally, you sit knee-to-knee, look each other in the eye, and say nothing with words, but everything with your eyes and heart (through your eyes).

- <u>Get into Your Body</u> – As mentioned earlier, we're more likely to *not* be present if we're in our head. If you're checked (or checking) out in a situation, when possible, excuse yourself for a few minutes and go walk around the block as quickly as you can so that you're breathing hard (or invite your partner and/or kids to do it with you sometimes). If you know yoga, do some yoga poses for five to ten minutes. Put on some music and dance for five minutes as fast as you can. If others are home at the time, invite them to do it with you.

- Reflective Listening Practice – If you're with someone you trust, you can ask them to play a quick game with you to help you practice being present. Again, sit across from each other (or stand), and share with your friend (or partner) five things that happened in your day that you felt were good, and have them reflect back to you what you said, affirming with each one that it was indeed what you said. Ask them to reflect it back, by the way, in a tone of voice similar to the one you used to share it. Then, reverse roles. Have them share five good things from their day thus far, and you mirror it back to them. If either of you reflect inaccurately, you need to start over. By the way, doing this with your children, at their level, gives you extra credit.

- Listen to Upbeat Music – Using your smartphone, iPod, or tablet, take five to ten minutes to listen to two songs you love that are really upbeat using your ear buds or headphones. [Be sure you first let your partner know you're going to do it to get present if they've already dropped the hint that they feel like you're not). While you're listening, move your body but also choose a specific *instrument* to focus on while you're listening. For example, when I listen to Led Zeppelin or Rush, I tend to focus on the drumming (I love drums). If I were listening to dance music, I'd focus on the bass parts. That will help you get more present.

- _Bonus Practice_ – Where possible, get yourself into nature for a half hour. This rarely fails to get _me_ present, particularly if I'm in any kind of fear or anxiety about something.

Doing any of these on a regular basis will hone your ability to get and be present with yourself, your environment, and another person you want to be present with at a given moment. However, I want to address one other key aspect of being an invisible partner. If you're checking out from yourself and/or your loved ones, there are likely two other primary reasons: (1) you chose a strategy as a kid to numb out from what I call your "emotional body," so living in your head gets to feel like the emotionally safest place to be; and (2) you have all the skill to be present, but there's something you don't want to face honestly, vulnerably, and in a timely way. You're scared shitless about something and are choosing not to deal. What I've learned over my lifespan thus far is that #1 can be rectified fairly easily, and #2 cannot be avoided forever. Whatever you're choosing (consciously or unconsciously) not to deal with and feel will _not_ be denied forever. It will get your attention one way or the other, and the longer you deny or repress it, the more inconveniently and uncomfortably it tends to make itself known.

To rectify simply not knowing how to be present most of the time (because your survival in your family of origin depended on you being checked out), I'm recommending a book that works wonders when it comes to teaching presence: _The Presence Process_ by Michael Brown (2nd edition). The first 150 pages can be a bit of a slog to get through, but they are worth it in the end, as are the daily practices given in the book.

I will say one thing as a caveat: being present means being present to *everything*—the good, the bad, the ugly, and the painful. One's ability and willingness to do that and feel it all makes all the difference between a mediocre to shitty relationship and an extraordinary one (holds true for life, in general, too). In other words, if you're not willing to open up to feeling yourself through and through, don't read or use *The Presence Process,* because you're not really going to be able to be a master at presence until you decide you're open to it *all.*

<u>Stop the Lone Ranger Crap</u>

Another thing that I've come to start suggesting as a near-mandatory part of building a healthy relationship—along with a really high level of presence and visibility—is to have a group of deep (yes, I said "deep" ... as in "depth") people who care enough about you to reflect your brilliance, your beauty, your depth, *and* your bullshit back to you, along with fiercely supporting you in achieving what you want. In other words, whether you're a man or a woman, gay or straight, I can't recommend highly enough that you find a men's group if you're a guy or a women's circle if you're a woman.

One of the deadliest sentences I frequently (and sadly) hear from men in particular is "I can figure it out myself." I can't say this emphatically enough: If you truly believe that and stick to it, you're completely bullshitting yourself and destined for less of a life than you deserve. Oh yeah ... and your relationships will not be healthy in the long run and will be at a higher risk for failure (Can I make that any clearer)?

Let's forget for a moment that each of us is incapable of being completely objective about ourselves because we're too close to it. Our brains are also wired so that we're always oriented toward what's going to go wrong, which means that we all have a filter that's not altruistically oriented when it comes to self-reflection. We have an enormous neurological web of beliefs, experiences, attitudes, and decisions we've made throughout our lives based on early wounding that could be decades old. We also have—as one of my dearest friends once said—"a hall of mirrors in between our ears." You can add to that that we often unconsciously attract people to us that are going to be likely to love us, but who are also going to be attracted to us—at an unconscious level—because they feel safe with us and vice versa. In this context, "safe" often means something like, "As long as I don't really look at my deepest inner stuff and don't point yours out to you, we'll both be able to stay 'safe.'"

For those reasons alone, not to mention how relationship eventually brings up all your wounds for healing, having a peer group of people to sit with on a periodic basis (my men's group meets every other week, for example) that includes people who are compassionate but who also don't let you buy your own BS is essential. Also, if you struggle with staying present in your life—much less in integrity and accountable to your word—finding a circle to be part of that contains some people older than you that strike you as being extremely present will make an enormous difference.

If you're a woman reading this and you're in a relationship with a man who doesn't have this—or at least doesn't have some male friends who fit the above bill—be cautious and prepared to eventually encourage him to find a group that fits the above description. If you're a man reading this, you don't have to take my word for it, but I will tell you that not having something like this puts you in the heart of what is, to paraphrase Einstein, a real dilemma: "You can't solve a problem using the same thinking [or mindset] that created it in the first place." If you really *are* capable of resolving and/or shifting situations and issues that are keeping you limited and unhappy, then why haven't you? If you knew how, you'd have already done it. Any justification you may use to deny this is, in my opinion, pure self-deluded (albeit well supported in our American culture) horseshit. And, I say that not only from my years of working with people, but also from watching how my own process has worked. I deluded myself for years!

I always say that it takes two to make or break a relationship—and it does! However, I think of my clients Veronica and Charley. They had been together for twenty years and had two teenage boys when they hired me to help them reinvent their marriage, which was on death's door. Veronica had no sexual attraction to Charley anymore, and—like a lot of men—sex was the one place where Charley *thought* he could really connect. He wasn't seeing that (for Veronica to even want to bump boots with him) she needed to be attracted to him energetically, psychologically, emotionally, and mentally. However, his habit of coming home from work in a perpetually shitty mood, being angry, and spending most of his free time playing video games was achieving just the opposite effect. He couldn't understand what the problem was.

He would tell me, "I'm trying," when he in fact wasn't trying to do anything but what he wanted to do, and he was justifying it with a load of bull that only made his wife and sons want even less to do with him. When I'd coach him on things he could do to change it, he'd maybe try things for a day or two, and when they didn't appear to work immediately, he'd stop, thus further cementing his family's experience of him being neither present or trustworthy. When it hit the true danger zone, he finally listened to me and went to a men's weekend that I recommend every man go through (more on that in a bit) and then found a follow-up men's circle. Both he and Veronica credit the changes that course of action created more than anything else for why, after eight to nine years of having no spark or viable juice in their marriage, they are now like new lovebirds who truly enjoy being together and are emotionally and sexually attracted to each other again (and their kids are thriving more, as a result).

So, if you're a man, you can search Meetup.com for men's circles in your area as a starting point. Another resource I recommend is www.mkp.org. Search that site for what they call a "Center" in your state or area (e.g., they have a Center named "The Pacific Northwest" that encompasses Oregon, Washington, and Idaho). Click on that state or area, find the info for their "I-Group Coordinator," and contact that person to get a list of any "Open I-Groups" that may be in your area. They also do a weekend training you can read about on the main mkp.org site called "The New Warrior Training Adventure." I can't recommend this training highly enough. (It changed my life forever back in 2000, when I did it.) If that doesn't speak to you, you can get in touch with me through my website (www.yourrelationshiparchitect.com) for other resources that could serve you, including one of my own men's circles that are open to men anywhere in the US.

If you're a woman, you can check out www.womanwithin.org to find a women's circle and weekend nearest you, as well as looking on Meetup.com for women's circles in your area that you can go explore.

Is your relationship doomed if you don't follow my advice on such groups or circles as a way of developing and deepening presence? Of course not! However, unless you want to be a typical person in a typical relationship, built on a cracked foundation due to a commitment to staying numb and superficial, consistent presence is essential, and finding such support groups are not an admission of failure or weakness. It's an admission of being awake and emotionally intelligent.

I'd like to share a keynote talk I did recently on 3 keys to being an Evolved (and Evolving) Man that inspires himself (and a partner), which will give you another cut at how and why this chapter's material is so....well, material! Click on the link below to stream and/or download it.

http://www.builttolastbook.com/

Chapter 10

Avoiding the Relationship of Babel

Avoiding the Relationship of Babel

If you were building your dream house, you'd have the design done by a good architect, who would work with a good engineer and draftsperson to have a set of building plans done that would allow a crew of construction workers and trade workers to actually build it. For that construction effort to go well, you need a great project manager that manages the overall building project, and you'd have an always onsite construction manager to manage the construction crew. In other words, for it all to go well, it takes a great set of plans, a good team, enough of a shared language that everyone can understand each other, and inspectors that ensure it's all being done according to the plans. If all the players in the building process each spoke a different language, you'd end up with a Tower of Babel situation where no one understood each other and chaos would reign, and the quality of the finished product would likely be a mess. Considering the different ways people communicate, the fact that our conscious mind is the project manager and our unconscious mind (with its myriad beliefs, values, and programs that don't often match our conscious mind's agenda) is the construction manager and crew, it's no wonder so many relationships fail.

One of, if not *the* most essential, elements that has to be present most of the time to avoid having the Relationship of Babel (where, try as hard as you might, you and your partner just can't get aligned, clear, and on the same page with each other) is the ability and willingness to **communicate** ... and to do it masterfully. This is no easy task. Relationships fail no matter how smart or intelligent someone is or how uneducated and unsophisticated they may be, because great communication in a relationship requires so much more than just vocabulary and language skills. There's so much energetic, nonverbal communication always going on—our facial expressions, our body language, our proximity to another person during a "conversation," our level of energetic expression, and the tangled web of all that we *haven't* communicated in the past - mixed with God knows how many agendas that are actually present between the conscious and unconscious minds.

It seems there are a gazillion books out there that address how to communicate effectively. My intent in *this* book is not to be another exhaustive (or exhausting) encyclopedia on communication techniques, but rather to be an instrument you can use as often as you want to be able to design, build, and maintain that passionate, loving, and lasting relationship. This chapter (as well as the book as a whole) is meant to give you what's been field-tested to work well, as opposed to a lot of comprehensive academic theory that you can't use for shit when one of your kids or your spouse comes home and starts talking to you like you're the Antichrist as you try to figure out what you've done to warrant it.

Lest you wonder what the hell's the matter with you that causes you to struggle to communicate well—and to be understood well—this chapter lays out all the stuff we weren't really taught how to do well in school. Remember what I said in a previous chapter about how 95 percent of the ways we react and respond to things are based on subconscious programs established from the third trimester we were in utero to about age seven? That's frequently at play, not to mention that our initial teaching (or modeling) for how to communicate came from watching our parents communicate—or not—with each other). Before laying out some "real world" ways to effectively communicate—along with other useful considerations to be aware of when communicating—in a healthy and conscious way, let me add two important caveats, since having great communication techniques alone will not give you the relationship you really want and deserve.

The caveats are quite simple:

- Remember that actions speak louder than words.

- If your energy isn't congruent with your words, you're lying to yourself and to whomever you're communicating with. They'll be able to feel it, and—in that moment—you're not trustworthy.

It doesn't matter how sincere you are when you promise you'll do better at picking up your dirty clothes each day. You have to realize that, if you don't actually *do* it consistently, your partner is not going to believe most of what you promise. If that gets to be the rule rather than the exception, you're seriously risking your relationship. So it's best not to say something that you're not ready and willing to back up with your actions and integrity. Yes ... it's that simple.

Now, the piece about energy and congruence with your words warrants a bit more explanation.

Communication Is as Much Energy as Words

Have you ever said to your partner, "I love you," without even looking them in the eye when you did it, or said it on the phone while you were reading your email? Either way, the odds are that the other person will walk away from that exchange not really feeling loved in that moment. Why? Because you only said words that weren't connected to the actual energetic feeling and resonance of what you were saying. Part of it is because you're not really being present in this example situation. The other big piece of it, though, is that when someone says something like "I love you" and is actually feeling that inside, the energy ends up totally matching what's being said because the speaker's *connected* to the *energy* of what's being said. Without a connection of some kind, communication isn't as effective as it could be, particularly with a loved one. In this example, the "I love you" is actually rote, and your Beloved hearing the words is going, "Really?!"

If you're listening to your partner bare their soul to you, and you're looking them in the eye saying "I understand" while your mind is thinking about what you've got to do when you get to the office, they'll be able to feel that you're not really all there because *something* is missing in the *energy*. It's kind of like faking an orgasm. It can sound great, but if you know what it feels like energetically when your partner has a real one—because you're *so* tuned into them—it's not really fulfilling or trustworthy, no matter how good an actor or actress you think you are. So, it's incredibly important to realize that communication is a *combination* of words, energy, congruence, resonance, body language, tone of voice, and presence.

When all those factors are lined up together, it can make all the difference between you being heard as someone bringing healthy conflict/dialogue with constructive intent or being perceived as a hostile combatant/bully who couldn't care less about anything other than "winning" and being right. Depending on where you are on that spectrum will also, in turn, help determine whether you're trying to communicate to work something out or whether you're picking a fight. And, because perception is reality for the perceiver, it doesn't matter if you didn't *intend* to pick a fight; if your tone, body language, and level of presence and connection are saying otherwise, it doesn't matter what you *intended*. If you really want to be masterful in communicating, you're going to need to be as aware as you can possibly be of:

- Your intention for communicating and your desired outcome for the communication;

- What you're actually feeling about what you want to communicate;

- What you hope you *and* your partner will be feeling when you've thoroughly communicated what you need to share;

- What you're afraid to say (so that you do it anyway);

- How much upset, distress, or other high level of emotionality is going on inside you so that you can own it in the conversation up front (e.g., if you're saying, "I want to just have peace," but your partner can feel all that stuffed anger in your energy, you're hosed); and

- If you're emotionally clear enough to be able to remember you're committed to *any* communication optimally being a win-win for both parties.

- Your body language needs to be open and nonaggressive if you want to be heard fully. It can make the important difference between being perceived as someone who wants to work something out versus someone who's wanting to pick a fight.

I want you to notice that all of those things are mostly energetic and presence practices—being in touch with your feelings, being connected to your body, being clear on what you want to achieve (okay, that one's a head thing!), etc. These practices are important not only so that you can be sure to achieve what you want, they're also crucial for being able to feel into your partner while you're talking—feeling into their energy, but also tuning into their body language, their tone of voice, and the inflections and pace of what they're saying.

Maybe some of you are reading this and thinking, "What's this 'be in touch with ...' stuff really mean?" It's fairly simple. Right now, think of someone or something you love deeply. Visualize them in your mind's eye. Feel that love for them? Are you remembering meaningful moments with that person all of a sudden? Your ability to feel that love, just by thinking about someone you love, is the main thing you need to be able to "get in touch" with all the things mentioned above. Think about a time you went to a business meeting where there was a person or two that you didn't feel comfortable with before you'd even spoken a word to each other. Know that feeling? You felt that way because you were "in touch with" or connected to that person's energy. You weren't *thinking* their energy … your body was reading it and sending your mind a message that was along the lines of "Ruh Roh!!" Those examples all illustrate a native ability we have to tune in to energy (ours and others') and to our intuition, and to parse a bunch of body language visual cues into an initial perception of how we're going to interact with a person and/or situation. In other words, anyone can "tune in"; it's just a matter of whether or not you'll put the energy and intention into it that's required for communication to be effective and enjoyable.

<u>Intention Is Everything</u>

Too much of the time, especially when we're upset with who we're talking to, we forget we have control of what we say and the choices we're going to make and just end up spewing out verbal vomit in very reactive language. Now, you're human, so this isn't about being perfect (though when you do goof up, it's *critical* to clean up your mess as soon as humanly possible to avoid any lasting damage). What I'm stressing here is that being as clear within yourself as you can be on your *intention* for communicating makes it more likely the effort itself will be successful. In case you're wondering what I mean by "your intention," it simply refers to what you want to accomplish in the communication(s), how you ideally want it to be accomplished, and what kind of experience the person(s) you're communicating with is going to have, optimally.

When my former client Liz needed to tell her husband that she couldn't deal with his chronic neglect of his health and the impact it was having both on her respect and sexual desire for him, it rightfully felt to her like she might get from him a very touchy and potentially explosive kind of reaction (especially since he hadn't reacted well to hints she'd dropped in the past). I helped her reconnect with her true intention, which wasn't just to vent on him and release all her exasperation. She actually wanted to make some kind of substantive difference that would, hopefully, effect real change that could get them reconnected emotionally and physically.

So saying something like, "Listen, you fat slob ... you're disgusting, you're about as sexually appealing as a rotted grapefruit, and you better get your shit together or else I'm out of here," would be a bad idea. Nobody tends to react well to threats anyway, but even more damaging than a threat is shaming someone. Given the topic, Liz's husband could very easily feel shamed, get really hurt and/or mad, and either fight back or withdraw. (His MO was usually to just withdraw and get passive-aggressive.)

Given all of this, I coached her to declare her intention(s) for bringing it up and—in so doing—"setting up his listening," which is a very important communication technique. Essentially, it means creating a context for the other person that allows them to know ahead of time that they're safe, that you mean them no harm, and that the best way to try to hear you is to adopt a mindset that's specific to what you want to communicate. It lets them know up front how you'd prefer they interact with you.

As an example, I specifically coached Liz to let her husband know that she needed to have a conversation with him that had one central intention behind it: for them to be able to be much more connected to each other because she'd noticed how much she was taking herself away from him energetically, physically, emotionally, and mentally, which she found really painful. So rather than allow more pain to grow, she wanted to share what was going on for her, to hear what he thought and felt about what she would be sharing, and to use it as a beginning for trying to sort out steps that could be taken to begin shifting things. She also—to let him know how she preferred he interact with her in the conversation—asked that he not interrupt her while she was laying out her take on what was happening for her. She told him she wanted to hear from him, certainly, but to please allow her to just present her piece first without interruption or argument so that she could just get through it since any argumentativeness or interruption was likely to shut her down and send her deeply inward for God knew how long. Then, she assured him, she would ask him for his feedback and responses, followed by them beginning to sort out what actions could be taken to start getting things turned around.

Do you see the difference that approach would make to you if your partner set things up that way, rather than just bushwhacking you with, "Listen, you fat slob ...?" It's also important that, in using this kind of approach, you ask the other person—before you launch into what you want to express—if they're willing to agree to that request. If they are willing to agree to it, great! If they're not, then you can either come up with a different request or ask them to make a counteroffer so that you can still get started, but maybe with a more bite-sized chunk. If the other person's a flat-out "No," and it's an issue that's *really* important to you, then gently but firmly let them know that this conversation really has to happen for you (*and* the two of you), and if now's not the time, then ask them when in the next few days they're willing to do what it takes to make themselves available to do it. Don't give up on your needs (another useful aspect of effective communication, by the way). If you keep stuffing things, nothing changes around it. And, if you just override the energy and try to force your communication on someone, you're very unlikely to get your highest needs met.

It's also good to be honest with yourself about whether your intention is really to communicate to win and be right (or to not lose something), or to communicate for both parties to win together and move ahead in a great way. When you examine that level of your intention, you want to be honest about whether you're about to take advantage of being *really* upset about something to just clobber the shit out of your partner with your communication (and it's energy) to, essentially, dominate them and be self-righteous (or "right") with them. If that's the deal, you're trying to win a competition that your partner hasn't likely even signed up to enter. If that's what you're after, it's best that you wait, put an empty chair in front of you, imagine that your partner's sitting in it, helpless to defend themself, and just rip them a new one to move all that distressed energy. Then, go back to your partner and try to have a win-win conversation with them.

There IS a difference between trying to win versus trying not to lose, by the way. The former can have a level of civility and respect to it because you're trying to move toward a benevolent goal. With the latter, odds are that your shadow ego's having a hissy fit, which means there's shame involved on some level and that you're at a much higher risk of being so motivated not to lose that your ego will do anything to be more successful—including being more manipulative, nasty, or even downright cruel. That's a really bad strategy. If you're upset but still connected enough to your love for the other person and your desire to reconnect with them, then you're much more likely to be invested in a win-win for you both, which can keep any reactivity at bay and make the communication effort more adult and successful.

There's one last thing I want to say about intention. One of the most important intentions to have is to commit to making *any* communication—*especially* when you're heartbroken or enraged—compassionate, respectful, transparent, and vulnerable. I've heard stories of things said between two people who say they love each other that you'd never say to a co-worker or a friend. When I press such people on why they were so disrespectful and even cruel, they say things like, "They deserved it," or (my favorite), "I couldn't help myself." To buy either of those justifications, folks, is heinous at worst and naïve at a level of "Wake the hell up!" at best.

In the three plus decades I've been with my wife, for example, I have certainly had times I was just hopping mad and furious with her (which usually means myself, by the way). Yet in all the time we've been together, as I've said earlier, I've never once shamed her or even said, "Fuck you" to her. Have I said it in my head? Of course I have (but rarely, to be honest). Yet I've never said it to her out loud. Why? Because I love her deeply, and I have an enormous amount of respect for who she is. When you respect someone (and love them), you don't say that to them in anger or aggression.

I don't care how mad or hurt you may be. If you want a Built-to-Last relationship, you strive, in *all* communications, to recognize that *no one but you* is ever responsible for your own emotional state and the choices you make regarding how to address someone and what to address someone about. When you say, "I just can't control myself," that's not true unless you have a severe mood disorder of some kind, in which case both partners need to be supported by a qualified psychologist or psychiatrist who specializes in such things. Otherwise, be clear that you're choosing not to take responsibility for yourself and your experience within the relationship.

Fatal Communication Mistakes

There are tons of ways to really screw up communication—most especially by not being clear on what you want to share, why you want to share it, and what outcome you hope to achieve. Yet in my years of experience in both my own marriage and in being a party to assisting numerous relationships over the last twenty years, I've culled out a few basic boo-boo's that can quickly escalate from a boo-boo to a major "blow it." If you learn to avoid these, you'll be well on your way to being able to have a much healthier, conscious, and enjoyable relationship. Let's go through them now.

Withholds

Not communicating is the number one biggest communication mistake couples make with each other (and themselves, individually). With every single couple that hired me—after years of marriage—to try to help them decide if they were going to stay together and then redesign and rebuild a new marriage (once they were clear they want to stay together), there was one major common denominator: withholds. A "withhold" is literally a communication (or usually a series of them) that was never delivered. You should also know that, if you're withholding a communication for whatever reason, it will eventually return to you, and it will be more difficult and painful to get through than if you'd just gotten it all out when it originally came up.

I've had it confirmed over and over that it's what you *don't* say that eats away at a relationship more than what you *do* say. Now, I'm not saying that being transparent, authentic, and real with your partner's always easy or conflict- and drama-free. Nope. It's likely to be quite uncomfortable and scary. However, I can tell you that not dealing with stuff, not communicating your truth (respectfully, remember), and stuffing and stuffing shit until you have a gigantic elephant hiding under your living room carpet that dominates your relationship is infinitely more painful. And, if you stuff things long enough, it can get to be too late to turn things around, depending on how much has been stuffed into a big resentment-ridden container that has "Fuck Off!" painted on all sides of it.

You *can't* have a relationship built to last if you don't trust your love and each other enough to be able to withstand upsets and disagreements that ultimately lead to greater alignment with each other, more happiness, and deeper intimacy, even if you have to walk on some hot coals to get there, figuratively speaking. You need to try out radical honesty and transparency with each other on easy topics and build up to what seems most scary so that you can see that you both can handle it. Where you can't handle it is a place to have someone like me help train you on ways to get past those potholes. Besides fear, people share a common reason for withholding things (and, by the way, it's not good to withhold things from yourself, either!), which I explain below.

Mind Reading

Half the time (or more), people withhold stuff because they're almost *positive* they know what someone's thinking and going to say in response to whatever they're reluctant to communicate.

Take the case of Tracey and Oliver a couple that have been together for six years and have a two-year-old daughter. In the last few years, they have lived in three different countries for Oliver's work and are now in the US. (Tracey's American and Oliver is from South America). In a session with me, Oliver showed up in a pretty withdrawn, irritable mood. Tracey was tired and pretty flat in her energy, and it was clear that each of them would've preferred to have been anywhere else but at this session. I asked them what was going on, and they both told me stories that felt like they were bullshit. The energy wasn't matching what they were saying. (Remember what I said about that earlier?) So, I called BS on her first, and she eventually started saying that she was pretty hurt by Oliver's recent moodiness and his energetic withdrawal from her and their daughter. I asked him if he was aware that he'd pulled away from them. At first, he said, "No," but then Tracey gave him some examples that he couldn't deny. He then attempted to say it was not really a big deal, to which I called BS again since it clearly was a big deal to Tracey, which—if you're really committed to a conscious relationship—means it better be a big deal to him. So I pressed him. He finally blurted out that he was really angry and upset that Tracey didn't want sex with him, that she didn't care about sex at all anymore, and that he couldn't stay in a marriage that was sexless. That understandably threw Tracey into a tizzy. [Extra communication tip: don't drop a bomb on your partner unless you really intend to blow things up between you.]

After I calmed them both down, I asked Oliver why he believed that Tracey didn't like or want sex anymore. It turned out that what he'd been assuming was completely incorrect and that he'd really never considered the impact that giving birth and taking care of a baby with colic can have on a woman's libido (and energy level). Then, based on some energy I was feeling underneath what Oliver was actually saying, I asked him some questions that verified that, while he wanted sex, what he really wanted—and was willing to leave the marriage for, if necessary—was to feel *wanted*, period ... and, in his narrow thinking, sex was the only way he could be wanted. I did point out that being wanted was primarily an inside job and that a lot of his anger was actually hurt and fear coming out as anger, but because they told each other what they were actually thinking and feeling, they created an opening for each of them to discover what bad mind readers they were and to get clear on what was actually true, and they reconnected emotionally and physically shortly thereafter to much joy and satisfaction on both sides.

In my years of being with my wife, Sarah, I've learned that—no matter how much I think I know her—I can never read her mind and vice versa. Even if you *could* read minds, you wouldn't want to rely on that because then you'd never have anything to talk about!

With this boo-boo, the best medicine is just to not ever do it, or—at the very least—to avoid giving any such thoughts any real credence unless you've been told by your partner first that they're thinking/feeling what your psychic ability is having you believe you've magically figured out. Always err on the side of just sharing your thoughts and feelings with your partner and trusting you'll find ground that can work for you both (if you're strongly committed to that as a general value within the relationship). Lastly, it's also good practice to just explicitly confirm what you think you've heard from your partner by reflecting it back to them and asking, "Is that correct?" [I prefer using the word "correct" or "accurate" over "right" by the way, because it gives the shadow ego less to grab on to fire up into some unnecessary escalation.] Until they say, "Yes," don't move on to the next thing. Particularly if you're trying to work out distress and/or conflicts, if you move on to another topic before the one on the table is really complete (that means you're both hearing and understanding the same thing and have come to a mutually agreed upon resolution), you'll just re-bury stuff that you really don't want to bury again. I promise you it'll come back to bite you both on the ass somewhere.

Having to Agree

Some people seem to think that something's really wrong if you can't agree with each other when communicating. Remember that the first aim of communicating anything isn't to be right or to get agreement ... it's to open a dialogue, to be heard/understood, and to open a pathway for you and the other person to be able to understand each other enough (and to, hopefully, empathize with each other enough) to be able to begin resolving differences and appreciating what's in common. If you don't remember this, you can make your communications much more difficult and painful than they need to be by trying to figure out what you have to say to get your partner to agree with you. They're probably trying to do the exact same thing, in which case your communication stops being an avenue of connection and becomes an effort to try to persuade the other. When that happens, you tend to stop listening to what you're hearing because you're only trying to hear just what you need to be able to better build your persuading case.

The way to minimize the chances of this happening is to remember what communication's really about/for and that it's *extremely* unlikely you'll agree with each other *all* the time. In a really conscious relationship, you're doing wonderfully when you can honestly agree to disagree, compromise, or simply agree to align with something you can't totally agree with.

Agreeing to disagree is just that. You realize that you're just not going to be able to agree with each other, you give up any need to try to change that, and you simply acknowledge that not being able to be on the same page is not the kiss of death for anything other than your egos' agendas ... and, in fact, it creates an opportunity for discovering new terrain for possibilities you hadn't thought of before. Being committed to that organic nature of possibility after possibility showing up in your lives also keeps the relationship vital on an ongoing basis.

Speaking for Yourself

In the section on withholds, I emphasized that you put your relationship at grave risk if you make a habit of withholding honest, authentic, and bold communications from each other. Another bad communication habit that I see in a lot of relationships (including business relationships) is the tendency to package up all the mind readings, assumptions, unspoken expectations, and projections in a way that comes out of the mouth sounding like "You don't really want this to happen because you're _____ and whenever you say 'X,' I know you really mean 'Y.'" In other words, you're speaking for the other person, as well as putting realities into their mouths because of the way you're speaking to them about it.

Consequently, I encourage a rule, if you will (some may call it a boundary): at no time do you tell your partner what they're thinking, how they're feeling, and what that's all going to lead to, period.

Instead, *always* speak only for yourself, no matter how well you want to believe you know someone, especially your spouse. Doing the New Warrior Training Adventure in 2000 was the first place I really learned about "I Statements," which are statements that begin with "I." Some examples would be:

- "When you look at me that way and talk to me with that particular tone of voice, I feel like you're upset with me." "When XYZ happened the other day, I found myself imagining that ABC was going on in the background."

- "Because of the timing when you told me that upsetting news, I made up in my head that you were trying to manipulate a situation. Is that true?"

- "I experience deep disappointment whenever you talk to the kids that way, and I get curious about what's going on inside you that would have you do that."

When you speak like that and are effectively taking full ownership and responsibility for your feelings, then your average bear won't likely get defensive right off the bat, which is what happens when you say things like, "You really want to turn the kids against me, and that's why you told them that Daddy was speaking to them that way"... and you actually were speaking that way at that given time because you were just fried from a hard day at work.

Again, as much as you may have fantasies of being the successor to the Amazing Kreskin, you'll always be better off assuming (here's *one* safe assumption) that you never know what someone else is thinking, wanting, or mulling over unless they tell you that they are. So don't ever presume to tell someone what they're up to. And when you talk about what *you're* up to, feeling, needing, wanting, etc., you *still* will want to use "I statements." It's just such a safe platform for supporting each person to take full responsibility for how they're experiencing anything and not presuming to project that over onto anyone else. That, by the way, is *not* an example of walking on eggshells. It's an example of conscious, mature communicating.

Not Using Your Partner as the Movie Screen for Your Projection Pleasure

If you want your relationship to be built to last, keep an eye out for this major communications no-no. Before defining what "projection" is in a relationship context, let me give you a quick and dirty explanation about one of the fundamental reasons that we project. It all starts with shame. None of us escape our childhoods without some collateral damage of shame lurking around in our bodies, shame that often manifests as limiting beliefs and judgments about ourselves that generally come out as some variation on "I'm not good enough," "I'm not loveable," "Nobody's going to want to hang out with me," or "Other people can do XYZ, but not me," just to name a few examples. One of my favorite definitions of shame is "not wanting eyes on you before you're ready." Believe it or not, there's "healthy" shame and "unhealthy" shame. Healthy shame is exemplified by a comment like, "I did a bad thing," which is then followed by cleaning up whatever mess that bad thing has created, including owning your part in it. Unhealthy shame is when you think, "I did a bad thing; therefore, I'm bad." Furthermore, for shame to stay alive and in control (which, from an ego point of view, is the name of the game), it has to stay hidden. Shame lives in our shadow side. When you're triggered into some kind of shame attack, you get into a dilemma. You *feel* the shame before you can usually even figure out what that feeling's about. It feels bad. You don't want to feel bad. On an unconscious level, then, you want to get rid of that bad feeling. So what better way to do it than to project that feeling somewhere else ... almost like a project-ile! Not only do we want to project that stuff, but sometimes we want to blame someone or something else while we're at it, so we don't have to deal with it.

Let's go back to our couple, Oliver and Tracey, who were doing a *whole* lot of assuming. Well, it turned out that Oliver was dealing with a lot of professional insecurities, a ton of fear about their financial future, extreme physical fatigue (just like Tracey), and a deep anxiety about whether he and Tracey were parenting properly. With all that fear, shame, and guilt going on, the healthy relationship building skill of being vulnerable and sharing those fears and how he was feeling (more to the point, how he was *thinking*) with Tracey wasn't happening. Instead, he was working twice as hard as he needed to be, was fatiguing himself even more, burning himself out, and blaming Tracey for not being demonstrative or horny enough—not to mention being angry at her for not reading his mind and taking care of him in spite of her being visibly and thoroughly exhausted too. He let it build to a point where he was downright pissed off and started treating Tracey and himself disrespectfully, all because he was scared to share what he was feeling and doubting with his Beloved. So, in this one couple, you can see a demonstration of many of the conscious communication mistakes in action: withholds, assumptions, projections, mind reading, unconsciously dropping a bomb, and confusing maintaining radio silence with strength (a subset of withholding).

Not Being Authentic and Transparent

This is a short and to-the-point mistake. If you aren't being truthful and real in your communications—even if you feed yourself, and buy, the BS about trying to protect your partner and your relationship—you're going to tear down the very foundation you designed at the beginning, omission by omission, and that will lead to you both building a relationship that *won't* last. When you think you're trying to protect your partner from hurt or pain, you're really trying to protect *yourself* from your own pain, fear, and uncertainties. A built-to-last relationship is one based on a commitment to radical honesty. This does not mean, by the way, that if you're in a bad mood, you get to be an obnoxious, disrespectful ass to your partner and chalk it up to practicing radical honesty. It means you don't withhold your vulnerabilities and shadow; instead, you risk letting each other know (and love) *all* parts of yourselves, knowing that the biggest healing technique for the shadow is to keep bringing it out into the light, so to speak, and loving it into submission.

Please remember that, overall, no matter how scary it may be to communicate, it's essential that you take the risk of doing it imperfectly. The risks there are far less treacherous than those incurred by keeping quiet.

And to the men reading this, I'll give you one last incentive to break any patterns you may have around viewing emotional vulnerability as a weakness. If you and your partner can't trust each other, you've got nothing to build on. Nothing says trustworthiness more than being authentically vulnerable with your heart, mind, body, and Spirit. Furthermore, if you're a mess inside and you're doing the strong, silent routine (unless you've partnered up with someone even more emotionally shut down/unconscious than you), the odds are really high that your partner feels you being a mess. So don't shoot yourself in the foot by lying. Take the chance to have an even stronger and more fulfilling relationship by being transparent and responsible for your own experience and allowing your partner to really partner with you in a supportive way. If your partner's at all like mine, they often have different perspectives and ideas that can be extremely helpful and are certainly better than anything I've come up with so far!

Chapter 11

Staying Away from Unnecessary Change Orders

Staying Away from Unnecessary Change Orders

In a home construction or renovation project, change orders will inevitably pop up—changes to the scope of the design and/or construction—that end up costing more money. While you always want your built-to-last relationship evolving and growing, the kind of change orders I'm discussing in this chapter can be summarized and defined by this statement that I've heard thousands of times over the last twenty years: "If only s/he would be more [fill in the blank] or less [fill in the blank], we'd be happy and in good shape!"

There are *so* many problems with this perspective and desire, in both the design and building stages of a relationship. I'm including this topic in this section of the book because it's usually a very consistent player in our minds throughout our lives. Hell, relationship isn't the only area where we don't deal with it; it can permeate your entire life if you let it. When you spend a lot of time, energy, and attention on perpetually wishing something or someone was different so that you could be happy, you're missing out on what's available *right here, right now* while putting an *enormous* burden on your life and your relationships that could never be fulfilled to your satisfaction. I'm not saying you should never want improvements, enhancements, or growth ... not at all. Wanting those things is a natural part of a consciously lived life. (As Bob Dylan said in his song, *It's Alright Ma (I'm Only Bleeding*, "He not busy being born, is busy dying."). I'm referring to obsessing on what's wrong and missing in someone or something that's conveniently and usually oriented toward external factors and circumstances. Oh … and are you noticing that it usually seems to be about everyone but you (Hmmm…)?

A healthy orientation toward evolution has an energy to it of excitement and possibility that doesn't have anything to do with anything being wrong. It's about an organic pull toward "What's next?" versus "What's wrong that has to change so that I'm more comfortable and happy?" You feel very comfortable in your own skin—whole and complete, even with fallibilities—and are looking forward with nothing lacking.

In a lot of relationships where this "if only they would change" construct comes up, it's indicative of a nonexistent or weak foundation design. It reveals that there wasn't enough "discovery" work done in the early stages of the relationship—consciously discussing values, expectations, history, past successes and failures in relationship, wounds, the good and bad about your family of origin history, needs, wants, and desires. If you discussed any of those, a current fixation on your partner needing to be different from who they are reveals you didn't go deep enough. You did the "safe" or sanitized version of mutual discovery.

When you start noticing that you're frequently wishing for your partner to be different in many ways, it doesn't mean you can't still have a built-to-last relationship. It does mean, though, that you have some catching up to do that may seem very scary but that could be tremendously exciting if gone into with an attitude of joy and curiosity. So if you're in this boat, what to do to get out of it?

It's All about You

Here's the one place in relationship where it actually is all about you! The first step to alleviating this kind of thinking that's messing up all the good that you have is to accept the truth that you're no-shit 100 percent responsible for how you're experiencing your life and your relationship, regardless of the circumstances. Yes, if your partner comes up and slaps you in the face out of the blue (a clue, by the way, that your relationship's been in trouble for far longer than you realized), they are responsible for that action. However, how you *interpret* that action, relate to it, and respond … that's all on you. (I know. Don't you hate that? It's so much more fun to just make it everyone else's fault and responsibility.)

If you're operating at that highly conscious level of self-responsibility, then you'll realize that a great many of your upsets and your wishes that your partner were different would be all about something that you're missing, wanting, and believing to be deficient in and/or about you. My client Veronica is really unhappy with how inattentive her husband is to her, their home, and her needs. On the surface, and from a perspective of "it's his job to be the husband I want," it's easy to see why she could feel right about that way of thinking and feeling, given the circumstances. It was fun to watch her begin to soften her position about how their marriage's survival depended solely on him getting his head out of his ass and giving a shit about her feelings, once she realized that she had her own ways of marginalizing him and his feelings without realizing she was doing it. Once I had her look at the ways in which that was true, she began to soften and come into more compassion for both of them. When she started being more curious about what his experience was—instead of just trying to figure out how to change him—some beginning levels of reconnection began happening. [By the way, there's very little that can't be resolved and worked out from inside a deep level of relatedness to someone.] From that opening, he's begun being involved in the coaching that he previously was unable and unwilling to see any point in, not to mention already experiencing much more intimacy and ease with his wife.

The more you're able to consistently practice looking at wishing your partner was different as being about you, rather than them, it'll take you on a self-discovery path that will repeatedly reinvigorate your life and relationships. Get in *that* habit, which only happens through repetition for a long enough period. Don't ever stop checking in with yourself to ask, "What's in it for me to change or fix my partner?" If you start hearing answers in your head that seem to justify trying to change them, your ego has commandeered the ship and is steering you toward an iceberg. Also, always have one dear trusted friend—one who loves you deeply enough to call bullshit on you—to run what you're sensing past them for a congruency check.

A great way to practice this and to begin getting really good at it is, when your sweetie complains to you about something—no matter how much it may piss you off or hurt your feelings—look inside to see if there is any truth to what they're saying and share what you've seen with them. When you feel a longing for some different behavior or way of being with your partner, be sure to look at how you can give that to yourself first. Or, do you have friends that have some of the qualities that you're longing for that help bring more of you out in the open that you haven't been connecting with much for some reason? If so, start connecting with them and putting your attention on what it is that you so love about your partner that just got inadvertently swept under the rug.

The deeper you're conditioned to believe that the "Happily Ever After" myth is the goal, the easier it is to get caught up in constant fantasies about how your partner—and your problems—would be *so* much better if only *they* were different. Well, why did you decide to be in a committed long-term relationship in the first place? When such fantasies start occurring, there are several questions you should ask yourself in a very substantive, deep fashion. Before I share those, though, let me add one important sidebar.

I have heard from *many* women that have been (or are currently) with men who look at their desire for sex, affection, affirmation (being told and shown they're loved), support, help around the house, putting energy into co-parenting (to name a few) as needy, weak, annoying, and/or as just a problem in general. If a man or woman who is already quite comfy in their own skin desires things like that, and is committed to keeping love alive and present in a variety of ways, those kinds of needs are *not* dysfunctional. Going back to Maslow's hierarchy of needs that I wrote about in Section I, these kinds of things are indeed normal human needs. If you see any such needs as a form of weakness or co-dependence, then you ought to be looking at why the hell you're in a romantic relationship in the first place, when it seems you just want a roommate or a maid. It's when your partner's *constantly* asking for those kinds of needs to be met—with an energy that feels like a desperate "I/we are *not* in good shape if you're not giving all this to me all the time!" kind of energy—and not taking care of any of their own needs themselves that you really should be concerned.

Let's look at some hard-hitting questions you should be asking yourself and discussing with your partner from a vulnerable and compassionate place while owning that you're clear this is *your* stuff. Doing this allows your partner to have a better shot at being your ally in achieving the healing that such longings often lead to.

Are You a Bottomless Pit?

You want to look at what your history around being satisfied has been throughout your relationship and life. Desiring growth is natural, but wanting someone to be different from who they are isn't usually about growth; it's about you trying to control things in a way that you believe will help you be happier or more satisfied with you and your life. So, going back to your childhood all the way up to present day, what has been your history of being able to be satisfied? When has anything been enough for you? When you've achieved things you said you wanted to achieve, were you able to really let that all in and enjoy it? Or were you right on to the next thing/accomplishment that you *had* to get? The degree to which you get a lot of "Well, yeah ... that's pretty much the pattern!" coming up is the degree to which you'll be able to acknowledge that you're prone to being the bottomless pit of need, where even if you partner *did* change for you, you'd still not be satisfied. They *could* change, and you'd be right on to looking for the *next* thing you want to be different. If this is a fit for you, here's what I recommend you do:

- Own that this is a pattern and let your partner know that (even though they've probably already figured it out) and that it's one you're committed to changing. Then brainstorm together ideas for changing it (including getting outside help, initially, which it usually takes).

- Commit to a plan and a timeline for shifting this and use your partner and trusted friends as accountability partners for you to accomplish it.

- Start doing the inner child practices I laid out in Chapter 8, as this bottomless-pit pattern started in your childhood, without a doubt. Find out what that boy/girl inside really needs, and don't be shy about asking them if they have *any* idea what it would take to be able to trust that they're loved and loveable all the time.

- As mentioned in Chapter 9 on living with an invisible partner, find or create a support circle of men, women, or both to help you with this process (and to help you stick with it).

- If you have *any* kind of spiritual path that matters to you, that pit inside can best be filled by connecting to what feeds you spiritually ... through meditation, yoga, or frequent walks in nature, to name just a few.

What's It All About?

When I wrote in Section I about how relationship design elements are a lifelong thing, one of the most important things you and your partner need to do is periodically examine, together, what the purpose of being in relationship even is for you because pieces of the purpose—as well as the needs, wants, values, and expectations—will change over time. So if you're getting hung up in "if only they'd change" kind of thinking, it's a sign that you probably need to revisit the "big why" of relationship that each of you have.

If you want to have a relationship in order to be happy, and you think it'll be your one-way ticket to Nirvana, you're unwittingly set yourself up for a fall. Why? It's because no one is happy all the time. Plus, if that's the main purpose of your relationship, it's inevitable—I assure you—that you're going to want your partner to "make you happy," which they can't! They can *contribute* to your happiness, but they're not able to *make* you happy, now or ever. This kind of arrangement puts each party in the position of being the other's sole source of happiness. That's not good. It makes the relationship co-dependent. Is that what you actually want? Do you want a relationship where the purpose is to try to mold your partner (and your kids, if you have them) to *your* picture of what everything should feel and be like for you to be happy? Or would you prefer to have a relationship that's built to last, which requires four main purposes for the relationship:

- Growing, individually and collectively – If you're not growing, you're dying. Your relationship provides the perfect sandbox for practicing being present (a much better way of moving through life, like it or not), *seeking* growth opportunities, taking challenges and adversities as grist for your evolutionary mill, and being committed to not shirking discomfort or even pain to serve your (and the relationship's) growth as a core value. If it *is* a core value and agreement in your relationship, then when you and your partner are stuck or really "on it" with each other, it's an instant sign that there's some part of you that is being stubborn about healing and growing past old stories and wounds ... stuff that requires you to get help to fix it, not for your partner to fix for you.

• Discover Your Divinity & Reflecting Your Partner's – If you have some kind of spiritual path, I believe that one of the central purposes of being in a relationship is to keep rediscovering your own divinity through the eyes and love of a partner that's doing the same with you, but not mistaking *you* as their *source* of divinity. In other words, if you want to develop a rich emotional and spiritual depth for yourself, being in a relationship with someone is the fast track to achieving it because of the good, bad, and "ugly" that will come up to remind you of the aspects of yourself that don't seem so divine ... so that you can learn to love them, too.

• Providing a Safe Container for Connection and Security – For me, and for everyone as far as I'm concerned, a relationship can withstand a *lot* of tough stuff and dysfunction—except an *absence* of *connection*. Connection is *everything* in a partnership, and if you don't have that with each other, you're screwed ... and very unhappy. For women, this isn't usually hard because connection is second nature to them. For us guys, connection tends to be something that requires a fairly high level of consciousness, intention, and presence because we're so oriented toward living in our heads (the big one and the little one). I want to emphasize that I'm not saying men aren't emotional or feeling (go back and read the first paragraph of the Introduction to the book). I'm asserting that *remembering* and *choosing* to connect to that part of us can be very challenging for a lot of us. Holding the heart and Spirit connection between you and your partner as being of paramount importance creates the kind of security that our children need to grow up healthy, to know what feeling safe is like, and to always be open to feeling free to experiment, risk, and grow. Adults need that too. What helps that happen is to also hold that the fourth purpose of marriage is ...

- <u>Providing the Safest Place and Ways to Practice Your Evolvement</u> – No one is connected all the time. That's part of why the built-to-last relationship embraces conflict, disconnection, and shit coming up as nothing more meaningful than opportunities to *practice* doing your own healing, supporting your partner in doing theirs, and to keep learning ever-evolving ways to come back into connection with self, each other, and the Divine (however you may hold that concept) ... to re-enter that juicy, yummy, energetic space between you both that made you fall in love in the first place. The alternative (and this is the more common path, from what I've seen) is to conspire together—consciously and/or unconsciously—to avoid growth like the plague, to help each other stay numb and stuck, and to tacitly agree to never bring up potentially painful or upsetting things (so that you don't have to deal with *your* pain). This will ensure that you become roommates instead of lovers. In a conscious relationship, you embrace arguing, disagreeing, and fighting as signposts and sources for directing yourself to the next growth breakthrough.

<u>Live or Memorex?</u>

Over the long life of our marriage, Sarah and I have both changed in many, many ways. We've gotten a lot older. Our bodies don't look the same as they did in 1982. Our energy levels are more varied. What we care about most has changed (except for caring for each other). What we get our knickers in a twist over has softened and mellowed. When you're wishing your partner was more like Jennifer Lopez, Sharon Osbourne, or Oprah ... or perhaps you wish they were more like George Clooney, Keith Urban, or Justin Bieber, you've lost some level of connection and fallen back into that trap of thinking you're together, so you're both automatically happy. You don't want to make a habit of substituting an external ideal or symbol for what you want to bring out of - and live - yourself. It's very conscious and sacred to want the same for your partner.

When this happens, you need to do two things, one of which is something to feel into and the other is a simple practice that I recommend you do on a regular basis:

- Go deep inside and see if your gut and heart have decided that your *actual* desire to be in relationship is equivalent to a blow-up sex doll that takes whatever you're giving it, doesn't demand your best and love on your worst, and is happy to be stuck in the corner anytime you're preoccupied with other things.

- When you're pining for the aforementioned blow-up doll partner, start looking—immediately—at five things you love and appreciate about your partner. Then, *when you're fully present and connected to your heart*, share those five things with them, making eye contact, and allowing yourself to actually feel what you're saying. If you can't feel it, don't share it until you do. Your partner deserves more than some autopilot version of you that your ego and shadow think ought to fly. Do that before you both go to sleep. [By the way, this is a great practice to do with your children, too.]

A long time ago there was a wonderful film (based on a play) called *Same Time Next Year*. It told the story of a couple who came together once a year for a weekend, year after year, to get to experience how wonderful their connection was. They could do it only once a year because each of them was married and had kids. The connection seemed genuine. But the point of the movie seemed to be that it's easy to feel that early-stage infatuation and idealized projecting that we do when we first fall in love. However, the real emotional richness and depth come when you cultivate and nurture the core connection you have with your partner and embrace all the changes and struggles as that which takes each of you fully into that milieu of depth—depth of feeling, depth of experience, depths of being tested—that make a built-to-last relationship so built to last. It's *easy* to find something that feels better and more fun when you get to have it periodically. It's much harder to keep recreating that juice with "the same ole same ole;" but, it's so worth it when you allow your commitment to growth to remain a foundational agreement and core value in the relationship. That's the big-girl/big-boy panties scenario that stands to give you the biggest reward ... not playing it safe, living as if you're still a teenager, and putting your head in the sand.

Section III

Maintaining Your Built-to-Last Relationship

—————————•◦•—————————

Okay! By the time you've gotten to this section of the book, you've learned (in Section I) some key things to work with to be able to design the strongest foundation for your built-to-last relationship. In Section II, I shared what I think are the most important of a myriad of things to consider and practice to be able to actually start building the main "house" of the built-to-last kind of relationship on top of your beautifully designed foundation. I stressed that you must understand that one of the things that characterizes a relationship built to last is that one of the core values and agreements of such a relationship is growth. You both have to be committed to steady, regular growth for the life of the relationship (as opposed to the old "Happily Ever After" myth), which means that you don't allow yourselves to go unconscious and inert, believing that "things are good" is the end of the road.

Even when you buy/build your "dream home," you don't spend all that time and money to just let it always look and feel only one way. If you're in that dream home for a long time, there's the required maintenance you have to do just to keep the house in good to great condition over the years where wear and tear naturally happen. After a while, your tastes keep evolving, so you ultimately renovate or refresh your dream home with new paint, different furniture, updated finishes and materials, and—sometimes—renovations. In our culture, when it comes to relationships, it's gotten too easy to do all that with relationships by deciding that (a) they're disposable, when push comes to shove, and/or (b) if it just feels "good enough," that that's good enough ... much like saying that your house is good because it isn't falling down. Using that standard of care and criteria for excellence with your primary love relationship ... it simply doesn't work and it's beneath you (you just forgot that).

In this section, I'm going to present what I've found to be the most useful and important of many different strategies, practices, and tools to use to keep your dream relationship well maintained for years and years to come. (Keep in mind that "good" is barely the average to be shooting for. "Great" is the end goal I want for you.)

[As in non-relationship areas, when you're choosing to do preventive maintenance, you can either go cheap or go for the best. Before reading on, I'm happy to share a keynote talk about Preventive Maintenance vs. fixing leaks as they happen. Click on the link below to hear that talk.}

http://www.builttolastbook.com/

I'll be sharing about maintaining boundaries and healthy control, the key characteristics of "happy people" (and successful couples), and getting from the "Happily Ever After" mythology to what's really true bliss. I'll also touch on the need to be realistic (at the risk of being a buzz kill)—not every relationship is *the right one*. So it's important to also look at when is it time to strongly consider getting out of a relationship to make room for the one that actually *is* the healthiest, most conscious one you can possibly have ... the one you *deserve*.

Chapter 12

Control or Healthy Boundaries?

Control or Healthy Boundaries?

One of the most crucial things to understand in both building and maintaining a great relationship is the importance of, and differences between, having healthy boundaries and trying to unhealthily control someone and/or something (the technical term for this is "control freak"). A definition I like for personal boundaries is "guidelines, rules or limits that a person creates to identify for themselves what are reasonable, safe and permissible ways for other people to behave around him or her and how they will respond when someone steps outside those limits" [Wikipedia.org]. In my practice over the years, I've seen that this is one of the key flaws that create breakdowns in relationships. Either one or both partners have no sense of their own and/or the other's boundaries, or they assume that, because they're partners, they can cross boundaries whenever they feel like it. You each need to have clearly set personal boundaries so that you know when you're in or out of personal integrity, you are in healthy control of your life, and you're living as someone who takes full responsibility for who you are and how you are living your life.

A very common example of an unhealthy or nonexistent boundary is when you're trying to talk to your partner about something and they constantly interrupt you, and they don't get that that's a problem in any way. This won't usually happen because they're jerks, but because they just can't conceive of any alternative way of doing things. That's an example of *both* scenarios mentioned earlier. The constant interruptions aren't seen as a problem because the person interrupting likely grew up being interrupted by their parents and other family members so often that they just grew to regard that as normal behavior. For the partner that has few to no boundaries, they won't see that interruption as either disrespectful or a problem either.

In her book *Coping with Infuriating, Mean, Critical People: The Destructive Narcissistic Pattern* (as taken from Wikipedia.org), Nina Brown identifies four main types of psychological boundaries:

- **Soft** – A person with soft boundaries merges with other people's boundaries. Someone with a soft boundary is easily a victim of psychological manipulation.

- **Spongy** – A person with spongy boundaries is like a combination of having soft and rigid boundaries. They permit less emotional contagion than soft boundaries, but more than those with rigid. People with spongy boundaries are unsure of what to let in and what to keep out.

- **Rigid** – A person with rigid boundaries is closed or walled off, so nobody can get close to him/her either physically or emotionally. This is often the case if someone has been the victim of physical, emotional, psychological, or sexual abuse. Rigid boundaries can be **selective,** which depend on time, place, or circumstances and are usually based on a bad previous experience in a similar situation.

- **Flexible** – Similar to selective rigid boundaries, but the person has more control. The person decides what to let in and what to keep out, is resistant to emotional contagion and psychological manipulation, and is difficult to exploit.

Put into plainer English, boundaries—when they exist and are known—come in two flavors: healthy or unhealthy (nonexistent would come under this flavor, too). So let's lay out some examples of healthy relationship boundaries first:

- You actually *know* that you have a *right* to personal boundaries, without question.

- You know that other people's needs (including your partner's and your children's) are *not* more important than your own as a regular rule.

- You know when you need to say "no" and have no problem saying it without feeling you have to defensively explain yourself.

- You are clear on actions and behaviors (like being constantly interrupted, for example)—both yours and others'—that you find unacceptable.

- You trust and believe in yourself.

Here are some examples of unhealthy boundaries (be prepared to recognize a few or more of these in your own life):

- You say "yes" when your truth is really "no" because you don't want to upset someone (and vice versa).

- You automatically assume that someone else knows what's best for you better than you do, and you concede to his or her wishes without even thinking about it.

- You expect your partner to "complete you."

- You don't speak up when you feel you're being treated poorly.

- You treat sex as a commodity, or you treat your body as something that isn't worth being choosy about when it comes to who gets to touch and make love to it.

- You "fall in love with someone" you've known for only a few days or a few weeks.

- You abdicate any responsibility and ability to manage your own emotional reality so that you can be a victim or helpless, so that someone will take care of you.

I've seen *some* version of many of these in most couples I've worked with. For one thing, during the design phase of a relationship (if there *is* one), boundaries are rarely a consciously discussed item. They're assumed, or one or the other partner just figures they'll be sorted out over time by trial and error. If you and your partner haven't discussed boundaries much, or at all, doing so in the early years of a relationship (during both the design and building stage) will go a long way to helping make long-term maintenance easier. You should also periodically check in regarding your boundaries, to make sure that you don't miss any that may have evolved or changed in some way.

Going back to the sloppy—and boundary-less—behavior of interrupting each other, being with someone for a long time often makes it easier to just assume that you somehow have earned a right to interrupt your partner. (Often you'll tell yourself, because you know them *so* well, that you already *know* what they're going to say anyway, so let's just cut to the chase.) That kind of thinking, by the way, not only violates one boundary ("I deserve and need to be heard and felt") but also another healthy relationship boundary, which is "I treat my partner with absolute respect at all times."

Of course, boundaries only help if they're both known and then communicated. If you're not letting your partner and others know what they are—explicitly and before they're unintentionally or intentionally violated—then you're really not going to feel too safe or healthy in the relationship.

Whether you're in the early stages of a relationship or you've been together for a long time, it's always a great idea to write down or type out your boundaries: personal space boundaries (how close someone can be standing to you, for example), how you want to be spoken to, what your needs are, etc. Then, share them with your partner (or prospective partner).

Control

There are numerous reasons why all of us value control as a mental and emotional survival strategy, not the least of which is that the more we can try to control—much of the time unconsciously—as much as possible, the "safer" we feel. One of the most delicate ongoing dances in relationship is the one between controlling certain things (actually, *managing* is a better word for what *I* mean) and letting go ... to allow, to be surprised, to be challenged, to be titillated, and to avoid stagnation.

The irony of being someone who really likes to control life (oftentimes referred to as "being really organized" or "super focused" or "driven") is that it really is Mission Impossible ... control is really just an illusion (and/or a delusion, depending on the circumstances). In another chapter in this section, I talk about the importance of resilience in happy relationships. One thing I've finally truly realized is that the more I try to control (also known as "making things happen") things—to try to bend someone and/or life to *my* will—the crappier I end up feeling. I get stressed, I get irritable, I get scared to death, I live in my head to the exclusion of my heart, and I end up not having much fun or smelling many of the roses some people keep talking about! Relationship is always a dance between two people, and if you try to choreograph it too tightly, it usually backfires. It's much more helpful to look at and relate to relationship like it's an existential interpretive dance routine.

It's true that you've designed your relationship's foundation and have hopefully been building it pretty close to spec, yet here's the thing: Healthy building and maintenance has a lot to do with being able to be in and embrace the tension between clear plans and skills for co-creating what you want while also being just as good at being in a frequent state of *allowing*. Part of a built-to-last relationship gets maintained by having and sharing dreams and visions for the relationship, along with establishing new goals and directions you each want to explore, both individually and collectively. And, while you're doing that, (all the while letting yourselves imagine and *feel* what those could actually feel like to achieve), you both also need to be willing to let go of your attachment to *how* or *if* they're going to come true or not. Lots of times I think that "staying on track" can be a closeted control drama if you're not tuned into yourself and if you don't know your shadow ego parts intimately. One way to be able to distinguish "healthy" management versus unhealthy "controlling" behavior is a blend of intention and how your efforts are coming out.

For example, when you want to tell someone else— particularly your partner—what to do, how they *really* ought to do it, when they ought to do it, and then try to micromanage them the whole way, it's actually all about you trying to control *life*, rather than *managing* your mind (or your partner's, again) and how you relate to the course of how life wants to naturally and spontaneously unfold. If you notice that you're getting stressed out and anxious because of how your partner's folding the laundry or driving, that's all about you. Odds are (based on my own experience) that such well-meaning suggestions and directions on how to be or do are *really* about controlling. Again, I don't think it's often about trying to control your partner. It's about trying to control *life itself*, to keep *you* feeling secure and safe. When you let that bleed into your relationship on a regular basis, you're going to cause trouble in River City.

I've also seen that when someone's trying to control things—or you— they'll often do so in a way that often triggers unresolved feelings from childhood again (Dammit!). I worked with a couple recently who were struggling with the husband getting very irritated a lot of the time whenever he and his wife were out driving. His wife would offer route instructions on routes they'd driven numerous times. She'd tell him where to park. She would try to control almost every aspect of a trip, which started causing him to dread driving with her because he knew he was going to—in his experience of it all—be controlled. Given that he grew up with a very controlling mother, most of the time that his wife would start that control strategy, it took him to old emotions around his mother's dominating, oppressive energy when he was a kid. Then he'd "go young" and either get passive-aggressive with his wife, or he would just out and out rebel or get pissed off.

What I helped them both see was that she had a great fear of getting in an accident, so without knowing it, she was trying to control him and fate. She would do the navigation and bossy thing in the car with him to try to control the likelihood of an accident from happening. (To be fair, he did have some issues about being fully present when he was driving that he needed to get more awake to and turn around.) However, her control strategy only brought more tension. When he was able to hear about her fears, be compassionate about them, and tap into the truth that his lack of presence was causing undue distress for the woman he adored, he drove with more presence, and she—upon seeing her control strategy—started being able to relax and communicate directly when she was feeling uncomfortable or unsafe in the car.

To be fair, *all* of us are control freaks to one extent or another, in one area or another. What creates a lot of troubles in keeping your relationship well maintained is when the level of control gets to be persistent, escalates, is covert, and gets leaked or dumped onto your partner. As with most tensions in a relationship, they're usually not about the person towards whom you are feeling the tension, irritation, and judgment. They're about *you*. (I know ... don't you hate that?!)

So, what's the best way to turn control and controlling feelings around? Firstly, when you feel anxious and/or tight with a person or situation, ask yourself, "What am I scared of, and what am I trying to control to keep that fear at bay and controlled?" Often, just asking that question begins to break the energetic circuitry of the habitual fear and control patterns. Then, you can ask yourself, presuming you've gotten a bead on the fear (and you can use the two-handed writing technique explained in Chapter 8 of Section II to get to it), if it's *actually* true; i.e., is what you're fearing really likely or even possible? Unless the answer's "yes," realizing that your shadow has just appropriated control of your own ship, so to speak, gives you an immediate opportunity to start taking some very deep and very slow breaths, get present to what's actually here in present time, and decide how you're going to act in a way that keeps you congruent with what's actually here right now.

If your controlling tendencies start to show up as you being "bossy" (as opposed to being able to just make clear requests without any kind of emotional charge or baggage to them) and/or trying to dominate or shame your partner (or child, for that matter), then you want to realize you're being dominated not only by fear, but by judgments you have about the other person. (Being irritated or annoyed is a dead giveaway that judgment and/or fear's running the show in that moment.) So here's a way to start clearing that out and defusing where your mind is taking you (taught to me when I was involved with the Mankind Project):

- First, identify what it is exactly that you're judging is going to happen or might happen.

- Once you've identified what you're afraid is going to or could possibly happen, look at what the projection is that you're putting on your partner that's doing (or not doing) something that's really bugging you … and why exactly it's a problem for you. Odds are that they're doing something you think is bad or not OK for *you* to do. So, if that's the case, you're going to have a reaction to your partner doing it. Practicing owning your desires and needs is natural. What tends to be unnatural is believing that without shame or judgment, unfortunately.

- When you've figured out what your judgment is towards that other person, start looking at three factors that could be behind what you're experiencing or that are getting you into a perfect storm kind of emotional state:

  o Have you ever done what they're doing in one form or another? Odds are that you have also done what the other person's doing, but you either haven't forgiven yourself or haven't been willing to come to terms with the fact that you do that kind of thing. So you're project the shame and guilt onto the target of your judgment.

  o How much do you wish you were willing to do the thing that you're judging (but you don't), and you are jealous and annoyed that the other person feels so free about doing/saying whatever's bugging you? (For example, if you've been terrified to speak your truth without getting attached to what others may think, you're probably going to judge the shit out of the person your ego has labeled as a loudmouthed jerk.)

- o Lastly, what is the behavior/attitude that's got you triggered and annoyed reminding you of from your childhood? In other words, how is the current behavior triggering you into a bad experience or trauma from the past, causing you to want to shut that person and/or their behavior down?

Once you've sorted out which (or all) of those have essentially taken your mind captive, you can then start taking ownership of your emotions and thoughts, connect with any young parts energetically (and through the two-handed writing) to help them get back to a resourceful state, and then look through freshly cleansed adult eyes, so to speak, to see what's really needed to get you back to an overall resourceful mental, emotional, and physical state.

Another motive or strategy behind trying to control people, in particular, can be to try to manipulate that person into not just being a particular way that makes you more secure but also to just get *present*. While not exclusive to women, I've seen it be more prevalent with women when they're partnered with men that are—more often than not—checked out (usually because of how much *they're* not really communicating). They try gentle to incendiary persuasion and attention-getting strategies to get the guy reconnected, present, and awake to what's happening with them. When that fails, she'll try controlling the man and other variables that she knows matter to him simply to try to get him to wake the hell up and get back in connection with her. It's the dynamic of "negative attention is better than no attention."

The need to control life inevitably leads to trying to control others and yourself in unhealthy, unproductive, and unconscious ways. Because relating to life—along with your relationship and your partner (and kids if you have them)—as something that you believe you can bend to your will creates more struggle than ease (as it's taken me fifty-some-odd years to learn), I want to suggest that there's a more effective strategy. It's simple, really: it's all about you, once again, taking on the responsibility for (a) becoming masterful at using emotional intelligence to create yourself as a total beast of emotional and mental resilience, which leads to ... (b) taking full responsibility for your own happiness and well-being, so that you don't even *need* to control anything. So, let's move on to the next chapter, where I'll go into how maintaining your own happiness, along with the habits of happy and healthy couples, can give you the greatest likelihood of maintaining a truly built-to-last relationship, no matter the circumstances.

Chapter 13

Your Happy Place in Your Relationship

Your Happy Place in Your Relationship

---◆---

Before I rhapsodize on what happiness is and the role I believe it needs to play in this kind of relationship, let's start with an admittedly party-pooper perspective that is definitely an against-the-grain point of view but could save you a boat load of misery. Contrary to *popular* belief, *my* belief is that *we're not here to be happy. We're here to grow - spiritually and personally*. Now, happiness is *good*; don't get me wrong. However, as one's main life goal, it's *horribly* limiting in its potential to evolve us, on many levels.

[For an interesting take on the roles that "Happily Ever After" and bliss play in making happiness more challenging in a relationship, I invite you to listen to a keynote talk I did on that topic. Just click on this link: **http://www.builttolastbook.com/**

Focusing on happiness alone actually *increases* the degree to which fear, shame, and control end up running your life, rather than your most authentic self that contains every emotion and every perfection and imperfection about you. Now, imagine being happy is the sole purpose of being in a relationship. How vulnerable do you think you're going to let yourself be? How much risk are you going to be willing to take? How are you going to build the emotional intelligence and resilience that it takes to treat all of life as worthwhile and adventurous—especially the hard stuff that is truly unavoidable? Yep, there's another thing most people who work with me don't like hearing: As Buddha basically said, "Life is suffering." No matter how optimistic and happy you work at being, life will never stop being a mix of the precious and wonderful punctuated by some seriously shitty things like death, injury, relationships that don't work, financial struggles, etc. Besides the fact that we learn more from how we move through such challenges, if we don't trust that we can endure and positively come out the other side of a tough situation, we can't even know what happiness actually feels like and how to truly appreciate it. In that case, we'll just semi-blindly keep dithering and spinning ourselves in circles, trying to "make it happen."

It's easy to see then that—in the context of relationship— if you decide to get into a relationship mainly to be happy, you're also limiting the potential gifts and opportunities that relationship provides to help us grow beyond anything we could probably imagine during our first crushes as kids. We need the polarity of the dark and the light to be able to master being with them both, which makes us fully rounded and emotionally intelligent masters of life. Furthermore, if you embrace taking on your own role and power in feeling and being happy in your life, as your sole responsibility, the happy place in your relationship then gets to be the love affair you create and cultivate with *you*. From there, relationship stops being a co-dependent dance; it becomes one of two masterful dancers choreographing and living out a dance routine that's sublime to watch and feel.

Having said all of that, I want to be sure that you understand I'm not promoting misery. I was watching a TV show the other night where some comic cracked a joke about how—essentially—if you're a guy, you just have to resign yourself to marriage being all about trying to appease "the old ball and chain," and to expect it to be a one-way ticket to being with someone who's just destined to be a pain in the ass you put up with, in the hopes that you'll at least get laid once in awhile. Now, isn't *that* motivating and inspiring? It promoting the false and hugely disempowering perspective that relationship is all about how the *other* person is or isn't and *should* be, because *you* say so! I'm simply offering up that you'll actually have the happiest (in a conscious sense of that word) relationship when you focus on *you* living and relating to life as a generally endless opportunity to discover what brings you to an internal state of happiness regardless of any external circumstance and someone else's behavior (or lack thereof). Add to that an ability to be of loving and playful service to your partner, while supporting and encouraging them to be in their version of the same quest with themselves ... and you have a totally achievable and fulfilling relationship that is built to last over and over again.

What *Is* Happiness?

Positive psychology offers one definition of happiness that says it's "a mental or emotional state of well-being characterized by positive or pleasant emotions ranging from contentment to intense joy." Many philosophers and religious thinkers often define happiness in terms of living a good life, or flourishing, rather than simply as an emotion. Others see it as having a life experience that's more full of positive emotion than not ... an experience that creates subjective well-being through a blend of feelings of happiness combined with "thoughts of satisfaction."

There are probably as many definitions of happiness as there are positive psychologists, poets, writers, scientists, and God knows whom else. For this book, I'm sticking with the definition that it is indeed a state of being (*well* being) that not only is full of those positive thoughts and feelings, but is also anchored by a high level of emotional intelligence characterized by emotional and mental resiliency. While I think happiness is pretty subjective, in 2007, Dr. Sonja Lyubomirsky created a quick and dirty test to gauge one's "happiness scale," which you can take right now. For each of the following statements or questions, circle the number that you think best describes you (you can do this on a separate piece of paper if you're not the type that likes marking up your books or if you're reading this electronically).

1) In general, I consider myself: 1 2 3 4 5 6 7 (1 = not a happy person, and 7 = a very happy person)

2) Compared with most of my peers, I consider myself: 1 2 3 4 5 6 7 (1 = less happy, and 7 = more happy)

3) Some people are generally very happy. They enjoy life regardless of what's going on and get the most out of everything. To what extent does that describe you? 1 2 3 4 5 6 7 (1 = not at all, and 7 = a great deal)

4) Some people are generally not very happy. Although they are not depressed, they never seem as happy as they might be. To what extent does that characterization describe you? 1 2 3 4 5 6 7 (1 = not at all, and 7 = a great deal)

Once you've circled the number for each question that best fits your experience of yourself and your life, add the numbers you circled to reach a total. To know your "happiness score," take the grand total of the four numbers you circled and divide it by four. The highest happiness score you can get is 7 (if you gave yourself a 7 on all four items) and the lowest is 1 (if you rated yourself a 1 on all four items). According to Dr. Lyubomirsky and other researchers that have used this happiness scale, the average score runs from about 4.5 to 5.5, depending on the group. College students tend to score lower (averaging a bit below 5) than working adults and older, retired people (who average 5.6). Given the documented increase in suicides and the severe challenges that colleges are seeing in the mental health of their students, that statistic makes a lot of sense.

Here's another interesting statistic about the sources of happiness that helps explain why it makes sense to make orienting towards growth the top priority of any relationship: scientists have said that roughly 50 percent of our happiness is genetics, 40 percent is within our power to influence and change, and only 10 percent is affected by life circumstances. Now, with the advances in the field of epigenetics (which essentially posits that it just isn't true that we're "victims of our genes"), combined with all the advances in neuroscience research and application, I could argue (as a nonscientist) that we have much more than 40 percent within our power to change. [I recommend Dr. Bruce Lipton's book, *The Biology of Belief*, if you want to learn more about epigenetics.] In other words, I suggest that the key takeaway is that you have the biggest influence, really, on how happy you are ... and it's still an *inside* job!

I remember nearly laughing out loud when my coach told me back in 1996 that I could and likely would be just as miserable with a *lot* of money as I was feeling, at the time, not having enough money. Really, my thought at the time was, "Well, nice problem, and I'm willing to find out!" Sure enough, when I hit an income level in the late nineties that was, up to that time, more than I'd ever made before, I really enjoyed it … for a few days. Then, the worry about how I would keep as much of it as I could, and how I was going to keep making that much for the next 30 to 40 years, began to create the exact levels of fear, anxiety, and unhappiness that I'd had most of my life before then. It turns out that there's actually a scientific term for that called "hedonic adaptation" (Google it if you want to know more), which essentially states that, as a person makes more money, "expectations and desires rise in tandem, which results in no permanent gain in happiness" [Drs. Brickman & Campbell, 1971]. In the late nineties, British psychologist Dr. Michael Eysenck modified this with the "hedonic treadmill theory," which compares the pursuit of happiness to a person on a treadmill, who has to keep working just to stay in the same place.

Now, I'm not a scientific happiness expert. However, as someone who resisted the idea for years that happiness was an inside job, I think it's extremely useful to consider embracing the research that has shown that there is *so* much we can do ourselves (and really *have* to, when you get down to it).

My younger son, who's in his late twenties now, is one of my most inspiring examples of this. When he was in the latter stages of high school, and then throughout his undergraduate and graduate school experiences, he was strongly challenged with managing his moods. For much of that time, even as he got better at managing his state, his greatest levels of distress and anxiety were rooted in either external circumstances that he wanted to control (and couldn't) or in worrying about what kinds of things were or weren't going to happen and what that would mean for him. Try as hard as we could to show him how that was fruitless and counterproductive, and that it was causing his suffering, he just couldn't get it—until a light bulb went on for him a couple years ago. (Some words to the wise, by the way, from another former mentor of mine: "We don't get it until we get it!")

He is now consistently in more positive mood states and frame of mind—as much as I've ever known him to be, even when challenges happen. When my wife and I asked him to what he attributes that, he said, "Stress management," which for him meant quitting smoking (feeling healthy is definitely a major factor in being a happier person), taking full responsibility for his state of mind and being, some spiritual practices, and putting a lot of energy into choosing to accentuate and focus on the positives more than the negatives.

If you're wondering by now what the hell all this has to do with a great relationship, it has *everything* to do with it. You've probably heard that expression, "If Mama ain't happy, ain't nobody happy!" Well, if you're not managing and creating your own emotional state (which, of course, is unique to each of us), then you're saddling your relationship with a weight and burden that few relationships, if any, can sustain and still be healthy. So you can see, I hope, that one of *the* most singularly crucial steps to healthy relationship maintenance is to develop habits that optimize your sense of happiness and well-being that you get to share with, and model to, your partner rather than unconsciously expecting that they're going to do it for you.

<u>Happy Habits for Humans</u>

While there are too many habits that researchers have found contribute to one's state of happiness to discuss here, let me share what I've found to be key ones, based on my own experiences and those of many of my clients. If you already embrace and practice any of these, you're on a healthy, conscious path to long-term success in your relationship! If you're struggling with being able to experience a predominantly happy state and way of being with life (and you've gotten help to be sure you're not suffering from a serious biochemical imbalance), then any of these habits should start steering you in the right direction. Before I get to the aforementioned habits, let me point out that I'm not meaning to contradict my earlier assertion that we're not here to be happy but to grow or evolve. I've just found that it is completely possible to feel in a resourceful, positive state (even feeling happy) in the face of a trying circumstance, through our ability to directly influence our brain. Shit will still happen, and needs to for our evolution. However, suffering with it all is pretty optional. If you want to see a living example of what I'm saying, get ahold of the documentary about Ram Dass called, "Fierce Grace," and you'll see exactly what I'm talking about.

So, here are some of the habits I was referring to earlier:

- <u>Smiling</u> – A lot of research has shown that genuine, authentic smiling increases happiness levels (and productivity, by the way). The smile has to be completely sincere. The corners of your mouth have to go up, your eyes must be slightly narrowed, the small crow's feet wrinkles should appear in the corners of your eyes, and the upper half of your cheeks need to rise.

- Cultivating Resilience – "Resilience" here refers to our ability to cope with adversity and adapt when things are going poorly. As I said earlier, being happy is kind of the booby prize. When you become extremely resilient, you have a much more fulfilling and happy life (and relationship) because you're truly who you are and you're fully self-sustaining, making love and all the other goodies icing on the cake, not the cake itself. From a brain standpoint, resilience is our ability to go from reptilian, primitive ways of interpreting and responding to things to what's called "high-order brain functioning." Some elements of resilience are: (1) the ability to regulate your emotions (including being able to stay focused and centered in the face of adversity); (2) having strong impulse control; (3) being able to analyze what's really going on when your mind wants to take you down the rabbit hole of distress (remember that you are not your thoughts and that you can choose to shift your state at any time … it just takes practice); 4) having good self-efficacy (a fancy way of saying that you know that you're on top of a sense of your own mastery and competence); and (5) you have a strong ability to be realistically optimistic, which means that even when things are going south in some way, you believe that you can manage your life in spite of them in a way that's grounded in reality.

  If you want to see an example of resilience embodied by someone who proves that this skill isn't contingent on physical maturity or age, go to YouTube and watch the video of then-sixteen-year-old Nobel Peace Prize winner Malala Yousafzai addressing the UN General Assembly after recovering from being shot in the head by the Taliban in her classroom. She embodies not only resilience, but also compassion, another critical component of having and maintaining the kind of relationship I'm talking about here. Without a commitment to living, listening, and speaking with compassion—no matter how upset or hurt you may be—you make having a built-to-last relationship so much harder and less fulfilling.

- <u>Healthy Habits and Healthy Be-ing</u> – Happier people also take care of themselves. They practice stress management (exercise and daily meditation of some kind are great for helping this along), they eat well, they exercise most every day, they get good sleep (Google "sleep hygiene" if you want to find some great tips for how to get more and better sleep), and they do what they can to keep their mindsets in good shape.

- <u>Healthy and Positive Moods and Thoughts</u> – This is (in my own experience) both the hardest (sometimes!) and the most crucial of the habits to work on to experience happier moods. Again, barring any true biochemical imbalances that may be affecting your moods and your ability to regulate them (in which case I recommend you get help from a combination of a psychiatrist, a psychotherapist, and either a nutritionist and/or a naturopath), you have an astonishing capacity to manage and set your moods and thoughts. You can learn and practice:

  o <u>Acquired Optimism</u> - "Acquired optimism" is where you literally *practice* the habit of optimistic thinking, which improves sleep, elevates mood, and reduces worry. This is indeed a matter of *practicing* (Did I mention that practice is *everything!*?) being present enough to consciously notice your thoughts. If they're skewing negatively and full of worrying, you can immediately start thinking what Esther Hicks, in her books and channelings of Abraham, terms "a better-feeling thought". For example, if you're in the middle of your day and you notice that you're fretting about how you haven't heard from your new girlfriend for a few hours, you can start thinking, "I'm so lucky to have a wonderful woman that I'm getting to know and that I get to be with tonight!" I can assure you, from my own experience, that this works.

o <u>Self-Awareness</u> – You must consciously develop an attitude of self-awareness. This is perhaps even more important than practicing. If you don't know yourself (and, tragically, many people don't and think they do) inside and out—mentally, physically, emotionally, and spiritually—you're going to find it very difficult to be consistently *at the cause* of your happiness and fulfillment in anything. I wrote earlier in the book about some ways to develop and expand your awareness of the differences (as my beloved business coach, Ronda Wada, taught me) between your truth and your training. The more you get clear on those differences, the more you're at the cause for your state of being, rather than the more typical "Why is this shit continuing to happen to me?" approach to relating to your emotional and mental states.

o <u>Staying Present</u> – A lot of non-biochemically caused depression is exacerbated by the mental habit of either looking back or constantly trying to predict and control the future with a default assumption that things probably won't get any better. Staying present doesn't mean everything will always be hunky-dory, but it does hugely impact your ability to stay positive, especially when it seems like the shit is hitting the fan.

o <u>Getting Clear on Your Automatic Negative Thoughts</u> – I named one of my younger, inner family parts "Chicken Little." It's fundamentally a chronic worrier part, taught to me by my mom. She had a PhD in worrying, and a lot of that rubbed off on me as a kid. So when Chicken Little is activated at any given time, automatic thoughts come up (for me to notice and shift immediately), such as, "Well, they liked this talk, but I know the new one I've got to give next week is probably not going to go over so well, since it's brand new and I haven't tested it 100 times first to be sure it's good!" Some other examples of automatic negative thoughts are (1) concentrating on the negatives while ignoring the positives (sound familiar, does it?); (2) ignoring important information that definitively contradicts your negative view of a situation ("No one likes me" even though 100 people called to wish you happy birthday); (3) overgeneralizing things, where you come to a general conclusion—based on one incident of something—that it's *always* or *never* going to be like that ("She didn't want to go out with me, so I'm doomed to be single my whole life"); (4) all-or-nothing/black-or-white thinking, where there's *no* middle ground ("She liked the dinner I made her, but she didn't kiss me afterwards, so she clearly doesn't care about me"); (5) personalizing everything and making everything about you and/or your fault ("Jeez, Shirley's in a pretty funky mood; I wonder what I did wrong?"); and (6) catastrophizing things and jumping right to the conclusion that it's only the beginning ("If I don't make her orgasm tonight, she's never going to want to have sex with me again.")

o <u>Accepting that Shit Happens and It Isn't Always about You</u> – As I mentioned earlier, Buddha reminded us that life has a lot of suffering. Trying to strive for a life without struggle and pain is futile and foolish. The more we embrace and accept the fact that bad or annoying things happen, and that challenges are equally as inevitable, the happier we'll actually be able to keep ourselves. Why? Because, we'll move through that negative stuff with a positivity that isn't *false* positivity, but more a sincere knowing that you've gotten through many tough things already; you'll get through this current situation with flying colors. It also helps to remember that *everyone* goes through hard times at one point or another, so when it's *your* turn, you don't have to go down the road of "How come bad things only happen to me?!" That also, by the way, will help you be a better partner when your significant other is going through *their* struggles.

o   <u>Changing Your Habits</u> – Years ago, when I was being taught about how the brain is wired to find and maintain patterns, I was given two of my favorite exercises: to spend a day wearing my shoes on the opposite feet, and, when showering, to deliberately wash in a different pattern or order than I normally do. Both of these were a *trip*! At first, I was irritated. The more I did them, though, the funnier it got, seeing how habituated I really was and how weird it felt to do both of those things differently than I normally did. However, it made me enormously present, and it showed me that I could acclimate (at least to the showering piece) pretty quickly. Happier people frequently challenge and change their patterns, just like *you* can (which also applies to communication and behavior patterns you're used to doing in your relationships).

- o <u>Dealing with Your Pessimistic Beliefs</u> – Beliefs are usually not just patterns; they're also formed by attitudes and decisions we made and adopted years ago that run in our unconscious background. If pessimistic ones (and the reptilian brain is pretty hardwired to focus on the negative, for self-protection) are running rampant, you can distract yourself from them by thinking of something else more positive; writing them down on paper to get them out of your head; disputing them (by thinking of anecdotal evidence that proves these thoughts aren't even true); coming up with accurate alternatives (like realizing that, even though six of your undergraduate students gave you a negative evaluation—which you're fixating on—194 gave you glowing evaluations); decatastrophizing the thoughts; and simply realizing how useful it is to stay fixated on the pessimistic view of things (Not!) and how destructive it gets to focus on beliefs that don't serve or work for you anymore, if they ever did.

- <u>Practicing Expressing Your Needs</u> – One of the tricks to this "happy habit" is to overcome any childhood wounding that led you to believe that you had no needs so that you can reclaim and own the ones you do have. Presuming you've identified the most important needs to you, you need to share them with all the people you love, but especially your partner.

- <u>Being Assertive in a Healthy Way</u> – This habit centers around your willingness and ability to (1) stand up for your rights (and express them) even though some people may not like it; (2) believe that you deserve to be treated with respect, compassion, and empathy; and (3) stop apologizing for everything, if you have that habit. This is not to say that you should dominate someone else with your needs. It *is* saying, though, that you'll be happier when you really can own that your needs and feelings are not *more* important than anyone else's, but they are *as* important ... and you stand for yourself in that regard without apology. This also means that you are able to receive others' feedback positively.

- <u>Vulnerability</u> – Check out Dr. Brene Brown's books, *The Gifts of Imperfection* and *Daring Greatly* to learn some of my favorite perspectives on the importance of practicing vulnerability to live a happy, whole-hearted (her term) life. For right here, I'll say that vulnerability means that you go through your life being authentic (in every way), open-hearted, and transparent with your thoughts and feelings; mastering being a great listener (and reflector back); and asking for and receiving support when you're struggling—with pride, open-mindedness, and with courage (for a lot of men, it takes a tremendous amount of courage to be vulnerable ... and you have to walk through vulnerability to even get to courage).

If you learn, practice, and refine all of these habits with yourself first and then with others, you truly can have a much more peaceful and happy relationship with life and yourself. When you focus on that (which automatically leads to growth, in my experience), you have way more to bring to another person committed to practicing and living that same kind of relationship with themselves. What can come from sharing that journey and process together is, quite simply, a relationship built to last!

Chapter 14

Getting Your Priorities Straight

Getting Your Priorities Straight

When it comes to maintaining your relationship in the best possible ways, it is crucial to remember that you, your partner, and the relationship are *all* organic. In this context, that means that all three of those moving parts (and, if you're parents, you need to add that in, too) are in a steady state of evolution and growth. In other words (as has been said for a long time), the only constant is change. We humans seem to have a tough time with change, even when we say out loud that we want it. The shadow side of the ego has issues with change and will often resist it. Our unconscious parts get uncomfortable with change and often resist and fight it ... and do so under the radar of our awareness 95 percent of the time.

Given those variables, one thing that can help keep you fairly stable and on course with those changes that your Spirit is calling you into is to be clear about your most essential priorities. To be sure, it's pretty important that you know what your key values are in life (and relationship) to help you make the gazillion choices we all get to make each day. However, priorities are not values. While they are certainly strongly informed by our values, they are the order of importance you set for your values, your to-do's, and your strategies for wish fulfillment on a conscious level. Because this is a book about how to be conscious in relationship, I would suggest your top priority for your relationship be that it is always contributing to, and serving the expansion of, each of you consciously creating and evolving your lives.

One reason so many relationships break down is that couples lose track of their individual and collective priorities over time, largely (in my experience) because time makes it easier to take each other for granted and to give the ego the time it loves to just settle back into old patterns of familiarity and pseudo-comfort. This is why it's useful to have another key priority be staying consistent with practices that you've committed to yourselves and each other to do for your own self-growth and the growth of the relationship. Because trust deepens the more people stay in integrity with their word, this priority has added value! You really would be wise to remember that there is no such thing as hitting a level of consciousness and life-skill mastery where you finally get to not have problems anymore and don't have any more "issues." There's no real place where you can say, "I've arrived, I'm done working on myself, and I can just coast from now on!"

A priority that comes most to mind that makes all the difference in the world is to actually get clear on what priority each of your relationships occupy. In Section I, I spoke about the notion that our top priority—in terms of relationship—has to be our relationship with ourselves. Then, if you have a partner, your love relationship would be the second-highest priority. Following *that*, the next most important priority would be your children, followed by your work in the world.

I'm aware that many men, myself included, were conditioned to invert that hierarchy of priorities: first work, then kids, then marriage, and then self. Statistics on divorce and the percentage of kids and teens that are struggling with self-esteem, their value, their place in the world, and how to really make it "in the real world" all seem to make the case that that inverted order hasn't truly been working.

If you're bringing a deep level of self-love, conscious sovereignty, and self-reliance to the party, and if you have a partner who's in the same or similar place, a built-to-last relationship can deepen that and can give a tremendous amount of support, safety, and mentoring to your children, along with giving you much more juice to bring to your professional life. Work is, of course, important, but if you have a crappy work/life balance going, it'll ultimately impact your relationship in a negative way. On your deathbed, if you have one, you're not going to spend your last hours or minutes wishing you'd done more at work, but you *could* go out regretting that you didn't enjoy your family more. After making work more important than my marriage for the first ten years or so we were together, I learned (and continue to live by the credo) that my marriage and family come first, right after my own well-being (they feed each other, actually).

If each of you are allowing your relationship to truly source your life, your children will get more of what they need from you because (1) your partnership will be an inherently great model for them for their future relationships, (2) you'll have energy to give your kids, and (3) you'll get to know your children from a different perspective that emphasizes emotional intelligence within and between all parties. (By the way, one of the best books out there for learning more about emotional intelligence is Daniel Goleman's *Emotional Intelligence*, which is now out in its tenth-anniversary edition.) Of course, there are a few other areas of the relationship terrain that need fairly steady attention and maintenance, and those are explained below.

Sexual Intimacy

God, I remember how awesome it was when Sarah and I first got together. The sex was frequent, it was hot, it had a lot of emotional substance, and it made both our bodies and hearts sing (in between bars of the orgasmic symphonies we conducted together). It wasn't the glue to our relationship, but it was the place where we both got to get out of our heads, we got to learn so much about who we were and what we liked, it really reawakened a lot of our most playful natures, and we also had lots of great conversations about life and what mattered.

In the thirty years since then, the sexual landscape has changed, as it does for every couple over time. I mentioned in Section I that that yummy and fun state of sexual infatuation we experience at the beginning of things is temporary (nine to about fourteen months). Once that wears off, you need to continually experiment and reinvent your sex life with each other, if you've both agreed to be monogamous. The longer you're together, the more important it becomes to be inventive and creative with each other.

It also helps to mutually define and redefine what kinds of things help each of you feel and stoke your intimacy, understanding that sex can be intimate, but "being intimate" does not automatically mean sex. Over the years, I've seen in my own marriage that emotional intimacy runs deeper and has more meaning and joy—for me, anyway—than sexual intimacy. Don't get me wrong; sexual intimacy is awesome. But with age, there can be physiological, hormonal, and pharmacological factors that either prevent or at least diminish sexual energy and/or functioning ... factors such as diabetes, andropause (male menopause), low testosterone levels, poor nutrition, and certain medications (like some anti-depressants) that have a side-effect of lowering libido. Should any of those ever happen, if there's a strong base of emotional intimacy that's nurtured in an ongoing manner, that's going to help a great deal to keep the fire alive, even long into your old age. I also want to point out that my years of working with couples has shown me that a lack of sex, a radical change in sexual interest and frequency, or even a repulsion to sex are not *really* the main issue as much as they're symptoms of an emotional disconnect (unless there's really a physiological cause) that, in itself, has to be uncovered and worked all the way through to a resolution where you both feel your hearts being reconnected. Doing that kind of work often leads to a natural desire to reconnect the flesh.

Again, because the scope of this book isn't to be a sex manual, I will simply offer some initial ideas that you can play with that can maintain and improve your sexual intimacy:

- The power of imagination – Role-playing and/or sending seductive letters or e-mails to each other can begin building sexual tension and anticipation (always good for the couple that has one or both partners on the road a lot for work). Remember ... the biggest sex organ is the brain.

- Incorporate toys in your sex play, including shopping for them together.

- Come up with creative ways to seduce each other, using all five senses.

- Change up the locations where you have sex (even going back to the car, for example).

- Schedule sex dates (vital when you have young children and teenagers that have a lot of extracurricular activities you're involved in). For example, schedule an evening where you go out to a nice dinner, book a hotel room for part of an evening, have great sex in it, then head back home ... as if you'd just gone out to dinner and a movie (which you could tell your babysitter). To add a bit more fun to this example, set it all up and take your partner on this sex date as a surprise (being sure to pack a little bag you put in the trunk with lingerie, toiletries, and a change of clothes for after the festivities). By the way, a lot of people seem to think that scheduling sex ruins the spontaneity and fun of it all. While there could be some truth to that, I can tell you that when you have kids, work pressures, etc., scheduled sex is better than *no* sex until you find or create the energy to create spontaneous opportunities to do the do.

- Break patterns – If you've gotten into a routine of any kind (positions, who comes first, etc.), change it all up. Do things you've never done that you've wanted to try. Share fantasies with each other and enact any that make you hot and are doable. Given the popularity of *Fifty Shades of Grey*, you may want to incorporate light bondage activities with restraints and blindfolds (whips or crops optional and to individual taste).

- Study and Practice Tantra – If you're not familiar with Tantra (and even if you are), I recommend you and your partner read *The Art of Conscious Loving* by Charles and Caroline Muir. If what you read appeals to you, find out where the nearest Tantra classes are and when they're going to be offered. If you and your partner have a good, transparent, and vulnerable communication with each other, that kind of work can take you to places sexually and spiritually that are a quantum leap of both emotional and sexual intimacy.

Emotional Intimacy

As I said above, sexual intimacy is fabulous and an important part of any committed relationship. However, if it happened that you couldn't have sex anymore, the best of what's possible in human loving is still available through true, sacred emotional intimacy. In my view, emotional intimacy isn't complicated when you share true love and respect for each other. It requires being authentic, having zero tolerance for withholds, continually practicing the highest level of communication mastery that you develop over time, speaking to each other at all times with kindness and respect (even when your feelings may be hurt or you're pissed—it isn't about repressing anything, but about waiting to communicate until your energy's in a place where you can be respectful and compassionate with each other).

I remember working with Bill and Christina. When they first came to me, they talked to each other with venom and disrespect much of the time. Each one blamed the other for their respective complaints and unhappiness. They frequently shamed each other and said cruel things to each other. They were so pissed off with each other and could be *nasty*. If you met them at a cocktail party, you wouldn't give them much of a chance for making it. However, one of the first things I taught them - and one of the first ground rules I set for them as a couple - was to teach them the red-line rule of communicating, which is based on an analogy where I overlay a car's tachometer onto relationship communication dynamics.

When you drive your car sufficiently fast to have the tachometer hanging consistently in the red (over the red line) and then stay there, you run the risk of causing serious damage to your engine. Similarly, in relationship, if you're talking and things get heated to the point where one or both of you is in your own personal red zone, you *have* to pause or stop immediately and take a time-out. Each of you has to take some time right then and there (whenever possible) to move your charged energy and then come back and continue. Why? Because in a dialogue between two or more people, the person that is trying to communicate something important while at that red-line level of anger is *not* going to get heard by the other person. It just *isn't* going to happen. When you're being spoken to by someone in that energy, all your young parts and your fight-or-flight chemicals are going to take over, because that energy doesn't engender a big warm and fuzzy sense of being safe. Continuing to talk in such a state is a one-way ticket to a pissing match that could cause serious damage.

With Bill and Christina, I had to get them to practice that *one* thing, initially, until they could get to a place where they could actually hear each other. Once they jumped that hurdle, the next step was to guide them into getting to what was actually creating all that tension, resentment, and hurt. Bill thought it was just that Christina had turned—at some point—into a bitter, angry bitch (not realizing or owning his part in contributing to any such transformation). For Christina, she was chalking it all up to his being a lazy jerk who didn't care for her or their two kids, who cared only about himself and his career.

While there were elements of truth in both viewpoints, what they were missing was how hurt they both were at the loss of emotional transparency, vulnerability, and an intimate confiding in each other that had happened. Once they saw that, it immediately began creating the beginnings of re-establishing that emotional intimacy that their self-protective strategies had covered over. When those were stripped away, they were able to get to the true heart of the matter, move all the stuck energy around it all, and start getting raw with each other about what it was they really wanted now, instead of focusing on what hadn't been happening for so many years (another characteristic, by the way, of happy people is focusing on what they want more than what they don't want/have).

This seems like a good place to remind you of something I emphasized earlier in the book: you have to own your own shit, behaviors, choices, and responsibility for your experience in order to build the safest levels of trust and intimacy with yourself and your partner. You *have* to be willing to not turn away from discomfort and pain with each other. If you can't go there with each other, how can you possibly be truly emotionally intimate and have the kind of depth that grown-ups hopefully seek?

The risk of getting raw and real with each other—with respect and compassion (have I said that enough?)—is likely to yield far more reward than continuing to suffer in silence and creating a fatal level of resentment and disconnection from each other. If you're a dude reading this, this isn't likely to be all that natural for you; however, if you don't learn how to do this, you'll just keep repeating the same dysfunctional patterns no matter who you're with. If you're a woman reading this, this may be much more natural for you, and you'll want to do the best you can to realize your man is probably not trying to torture you; he's just scared shitless to go to an inner territory that he's been conditioned and/or punished for most of his life to stay away from. So, in such a case, I don't recommend you let your hurt feelings keep you from going to your highest self to bring what's needed to clear the logjam for both of you. Who goes first is much less important than the breakthroughs that could be waiting for you if *one* of you would get off both your pride and the pot, if you get my drift.

While there are numerous other ways to keep emotional intimacy alive and thriving, I really believe that—if you had to choose one primary way of doing it—practicing vulnerability by sharing your mind, body, heart, and Spirit will certainly get you there.

A Good Balance of Power

I'm going to make this really short and sweet. One of the biggest tricks your ego-mind plays with you is to try to convince you that you're doing well if you're "ahead"—of life, the boogeyman, the bill collectors, and (when fear *really* has us by the short hairs) even our partner. In a sacred, built-to-last paradigm, there can no longer be *any* tolerance of, and room for, indulging a scorekeeping way of being that centers around who wins the most arguments and "who wears the pants in the relationship." There can only be *shared* power that coheres around what's most valuable to you both: your own individual sovereignty and congruence, along with the sanctity of your relationship being a Divine gift to help you truly experience *your* Divinity. So when you and your partner notice that all of that's being forgotten and going by the wayside, that's a sign you need to check on the foundation, make repairs, get current with each other, clean out the withholds closet, and reorient yourselves to where you want to go in the relationship, how you want to feel/experience your relationship, and what you need to do to get there. If you've let things go too long and it's a continual contest to see who can win over the other, you'd be wise to ask for help from an outside professional.

Where there's true power is in holding the health of the partnership as a paramount priority that sources everything (well, first hold your own well-being as paramount). Once you do that as a regular way of Be-ing, your relationship's foundation keeps getting stronger and stronger over time.

In the next chapter, you'll get to learn scientifically confirmed guiding principles and habits that will also help give you a basic road map for the best possible maintenance of your relationship.

Chapter 15

6 Key Pathways to Maintaining Your Built-to-Last Relationship

6 Key Pathways to Maintaining Your Built-to-Last Relationship

————————●◆●————————

It seems fitting to close this section of the book by first reminding you that a physical "dream home" that you live in is never completely static and maintenance-free for the duration of the time you live in it. There's regular, preventative maintenance, which anyone with any sense would fully commit to doing to get the most out of all aspects of their house. Then, if you stay in the home for a long time, there's periodic redecorating, upgrading, and updating aspects of the home (like the furnace, water heater, and appliances) that show enough wear and tear to make it clear it's time to update. For some people, as needs change, they may even decide to renovate their home; others may outgrow their house, so they decide to find or create a different dream home. Of course, there are others who decide to leave that dream home altogether, because they've decided it's time to leave the relationship in which the dream home has been a symbiotic partner. In a real housing situation, all of these create fun new possibilities, a sense of adventure, and no small degree of stress, particularly if you've not done much of this before. Even if you *have* done it before, each time … each step … each moving part … they are all going to have differences and circumstances that require a degree of improvisation, flexibility, and resilience—and *that's* if you're doing it consciously and proactively.

Unfortunately, from my experiences in my practice, many couples (and individuals) don't get proactive. They wait until wallpaper's peeling off, the hot water in the shower no longer works, or their partner has told them, "It's been nice knowing you; I'm leaving now!" Many people want their partners/spouses to read their minds, know their needs, give them what they want (but haven't explicitly asked for), and anticipate future needs. Too many people expect all that to just automatically be happening, even when they rationally understand how unreasonable that is. Such people wait for their partners to pick up on this and get in gear, all the while building up resentment for what they're not getting—or creating for him- or herself, by the way. However, it doesn't have to be that way.

While everyone's different and there's so much about love that's unique to each person (not to mention thousands of books, like this one, telling you how to have a great relationship and/or repair one) that makes a cookie-cutter approach unwise, we're fortunate to have some pathways that have been established through extensive, comprehensive research done over the last several decades with thousands of couples. Dr. John Gottman has spent the last twenty-three years conducting peer-reviewed research on what the most common qualities and characteristics are of successful (and unsuccessful) relationships. Over the last couple decades, it's been shown that his conclusions and predictors of what will likely result in divorce hang in the 85–87 percent accuracy range, according to Wikipedia. One of his most useful findings is that two variables, in particular, are present in the most successful couples ("successful" meaning their relationship lasts a long time and is fulfilling to both parties): kindness and generosity. (As an aside, think of how often you embody and practice each of those with your love partner and/or others in your life. That'd be an important and worthwhile assessment to make!)

Based on all his research, working with both couples and couples therapists, Dr. Gottman (along with Julie, his wife of twenty years and herself a psychotherapist) has identified six key principles of happy and enduring couples that I'm going to elaborate on below in a way that gives you practical, preventive maintenance steps and practices you can use to keep your relationship—and its foundation—strong for a *long* time.

1. Focus on the Positive

Listen, your shadow ego will *relentlessly* try to convince you that you should have better things, that you should enjoy things more, that you deserve to have certain things and hate that you don't have them. When it's applying this specifically to both your partner (how they leave the toilet seat up all the time, or don't make what you like to eat often enough, for example) and the relationship (things like, "How come neither of us ever seem to follow through on creating what we say we want and are committed to?"), it can get pretty confusing. To that part of the ego, there's no shortage of "The grass is greener on the other side" perspective. To make things even more difficult, we live in a culture where relationships have become way too much like easily disposable containers for determining just how far people can take self-absorption and narcissism to new heights (it isn't always about *your* needs, Bucko!).

If you relate to life as if you should have everything you want and you should have it easily, and others should have no problem making that happen for you, I'd strongly suggest you stay away from getting into a relationship. That way of relating to life isn't going to go far in building something that will last. I offer this observation and opinion, by the way, because of what I've seen over and over again working with couples, while also looking hard at why my marriage has stayed strong and vital for so long.

Our reptilian brain defaults to looking for where the next saber-toothed tiger is that wants to have you for dinner. You want to remember that's a *default* and not what you're doomed to suffer with for eternity. However, it's a sucky way to be in relationship, letting that part of our brain run the show. One way to turn that predisposition around is to consciously practice exercising your ability (and, admittedly, your prerogative) to choose where you focus your thoughts. If you keep looking for what's wrong, what's missing, and what sucks ... guess what? You'll find it! The good news is that if you're looking for what's positive, what's working wonderfully, what's exciting, and what makes your heart and body feel expanded ... you'll find that too! It's crucial, particularly if you've already been with someone a long time, to continually be noticing, commenting on, and reflecting to each other what your positive qualities are, the positive feelings you have for each other, and not only creating good times day to day/week to week, but remembering the great experiences you've already had with each other (which, neurologically, can help you feel those wonderful feelings again and start carving in some new positively oriented neural pathways).

An exercise I have my couples do is to share five good things that have happened in their day, on a daily basis, with each other. Then, once they get the hang of *that*, I have them look for and share three to five things they admire, respect, and love about *each other* no *less* than every three days. One of Dr. Gottman's suggestions is for couples to commit to a thirty-day fast from negativity, which is a tremendously enlightening and transformational practice, whether you're in a relationship or not! I encourage you to try that one. It isn't about not ever disagreeing with each other or needing to communicate how something could work better (notice how I spun that language, rather than "Here's what doesn't work for me, Chica!"); it's an opportunity to discover different ways of communicating it that can build more feelings of unconditional positive regard for each other, especially in the face of challenging times and circumstances. When one of our kids went through a life-threatening health crisis several years ago, it was our ability to keep finding the positives, even in *that* situation, that not only helped us help our child but to keep our relationship strong in circumstances that have torn many marriages apart.

2. Quantity *and* Quality Time

It's *crucial* that you and your partner make getting and staying *connected* every day one of your highest priorities. There's no question that it's *great* when it's a really deep, intimate, and vulnerable connection, in and/or out of bed. However, the way most people live life these days—and with all the demands on our time, focus, and energy—it's not too realistic to think that you're going to have that kind of connection every single day (though, that's not meant to be an absolute argument against bucking that trend of non-realistic-ness).

So, while it's desirable to make a good *quantity* of quality time happen as often as you can, it's almost equally valuable to create a *quantity* of bite-sized quality moments to connect with each other where you share what happened in your day (and ask the same question of your partner while actually *listening*). You want to share thoughts and experiences with each other, both mundane and profound. Too many couples get mired and stuck in making their connection all about logistics ... who's picking up the dry cleaning, who's taking which kid to soccer and baseball practice, etc. That stuff is important, sure, but you need more than that to keep a relationship alive. A lot of little moments—as long as they involve each of you being fully present with each other when they happen, and connecting your hearts up (even through just holding hands while you're talking and listening, or with open-hearted hugs and kisses)—can go a long-ass way to keeping your romance fueled over and over again. I don't care how busy you are. For the best preventive maintenance, if you do this as a committed practice every day, you'll get a very useful reward. If you're parents with kids at home, this is a good pathway to maintain great relationships with them, too; however, you must have some of these quality-time McNuggets without your children, too. Believe me ... they'll be so much better for it and thank you when they become adults in their own relationships.

I offer you a parting thought on this topic of quality time. A blogger I read regularly recently quoted Cheryl Strayed, the author of the book (that became a wonderful film) *Wild*. She said that she felt the one thing that *everyone* wants most in a relationship is *attention*. I personally believe that the number one thing all of us really want is connection; however, how do you connect if you're not giving and paying attention to each other? As I wrote in Section II, women will leave men they love because they're simply not getting enough attention, which also means they're not getting their man's *presence*. They're not getting that Divine Masculine energy that the Divine Feminine loves being embraced and penetrated by. [A great book that goes beautifully into the dynamics of how Divine Feminine and Divine Masculine work together is

David Deida's "Intimate Communion."] I can't overstate the importance of regular, daily attention—open-hearted, open-minded, and fully present attention with eyes, ears, and bodily awareness—being given to each other.

You guys who get hung up on quantity vs. quality in the bedroom or with your junk, here's the one arena where quantity really *does* matter. But if you're just providing a quantity of attention with little to no presence attached, you're screwing the pooch when it comes to quality. You ladies reading this, even though we guys can do the strong, silent type BS that a lot of us have been trained to mistake for character and strength, don't be fooled. Men are just as deeply feeling and emotional as women, but we are often inhibited and confused about how to be with it and relate to that part of ourselves, except when it comes out watching sports. So, I encourage you to not get discouraged or indignant when you have to draw your man's feelings out of him, at least initially. Any reticence he has likely has nothing to do with how much he loves you. It has *everything* to do with the deep wounding we all have, in one way or the other, and needing to feel safe to be vulnerable (even with you who loves him). It isn't your job or responsibility to make him feel safe—you can't. However, you can offer him an energetic container that's conducive to helping him decide it's safe to open up by being embraced by your Divine Feminine power, asking him questions with an energy of sincere curiosity and from a softened energy (i.e., really giving him attention and paying attention).

3. Let Your Partner Influence You

When you stop to think about it, is there any sane reason you can think of to be in a committed relationship with someone and not give a shit about what they think, say, know, teach, demonstrate, and model? Is there any rational reason why you'd be in the kind of relationship where you're the "boss" (or you let your partner be) and have all the power in the relationship? Wouldn't it just be easier to have a Zoomba and an account with Merry Maids? If you can come up with any good, even semi-reasonable answers to those questions, you either *really* need this book or should give it to someone who could really use it … and would.

Happy couples not only share with each other and frequently connect with each other, but they share power and get influenced by each other. Remember, you want to be in a relationship as a fast track to personal growth and evolution. That means that you never want to stop noticing:

- The qualities you admire in your partner

- What they teach you by how they interact with life

- What they model in the areas of social, mental, and emotional intelligence

- How they push you and others to be even more of who you/they are

- How they give you—directly or indirectly—a bunch of WTF moments that stretch you out of your comfort zones and inertia

- The opportunities they give you to collaborate with each other's brilliance to come up with numerous solutions to life's challenges while keeping your hearts open and staying deeply connected

The most successful couples I know are couples that truly like and respect each other not just for *who* they are, but for *how* they are and how they embody highly conscious BE-ing in their lives. They truly seek each other out for counsel and ideas. They don't get shy or prideful when it comes to asking their partner for their opinion on something they don't know much about. Each partner is also great about asking the other what they've been learning and what challenges they've been breaking through—and how. They also, when posed with a pretty large challenge, don't get hung up on who's got the best answers, who's going to be the most right or wrong in a situation, and who's going to look good in the eyes of whomever. They gladly and easily share all their mental, emotional, physical, and spiritual resources (internal and external) with each other to consciously create learning, growth, and innovation in all areas of their lives.

I can honestly say that Sarah has influenced me in more ways than she probably even realizes, -- as a man, a lover, a mentor and coach, and a loving human being. I know I've strongly influenced her in stepping more into owning her power; reminding her what a special gift her Divine Feminine really is to me and our children (and our dog, I have to say); claiming what she wants and needs without apology or doubt; knowing how to let go of worry; knowing how to put herself and her needs at the top; and knowing how to develop a fun potty mouth I can partner with. Part of maintaining a built-to-last relationship is to actively seek out ways that you can influence each other and share power even more. You should both check in with each other about this topic at least a couple times a year, at a minimum. Also, don't forget to *tell* your partner how they're influencing you. Even after thirty-three years, it still touches Sarah to hear how she influences me differently now, but in just as valued a way.

4. Solve Solvable Problems – as a *Team*

Firstly, it's useful to take a stab at distinguishing what problems are solvable and which ones aren't so that you don't waste precious time and energy with your knickers in a twist over something you can't change. For example, a solvable problem can look something like, "How are we going to sort out daycare for Junior given the new jobs we both just got?" It may not be *easily* solvable, but it *is* solvable. An unsolvable problem could look like, "I wish Betty would like all my Megadeath CDs" (when thrash metal makes Betty want to run screaming off into the sunset). It could be that a solution may emerge for Betty not running into the sunset, but you're never likely to get Betty to *like* thrash metal. That's unsolvable.

As I've said several times already (so why not one more, eh?), your relationship will stand or fall on your ability to not only make it your second-highest priority (behind being the best you that you can be), but to deal with conflicts and challenges as a team and as an opportunity rather than a liability. This means when you're trying to work through a solvable problem, you need to focus on the following things:

- <u>Admitting you have a problem</u> – Dr. Gottman's research shows that in both happy and unhappy marriages, more than 80 percent of the time the wife brings up marital issues while the husband tries to avoid admitting she's right, dealing with it, and showing up as a committed partner to do what can be done to give the relationship a shot. So both of you have to screw up both the courage and commitment levels to celebrate all that's good about the relationship ... and tell the truth about what isn't working in a proactive way. Once that's been done, you're ready for the next things you need to do.

- <u>Using I-Statements</u> – You don't speak for each other or presume to believe and say you *know* what the other's thinking and/or up to. You take full ownership of your own experience and perceptions and state them in sentences like, "When you ask me to empty the dishwasher in that tone of voice, **I** notice I start getting irritated," instead of the more common, "Listen, you nagging pain in the ass, you've got to stop messing with me and getting me pissed off by telling me to empty the dishwasher in that tone of voice!"

- <u>Taking breaks</u> – Like I said in the last chapter, if either or both of you are at a level of distress or upset that's taking you over your inner red line, you *must* take a break and go move your energy. Continuing to try to force something or get a point across when someone's in that level of upset … it just ain't gonna happen. Without a break, you're likely to say something you're not going to be able to un-say, causing damage you may not be able to rectify. Just be sure that if you *are* going to take a break, you explicitly tell your partner, "I need a break or time-out to go move my energy and get back into my heart. I'll come back to you as soon as I've done that. I promise." Then, whatever you do, keep that promise!

- <u>Remembering it's the behavior, not the person</u> – Notice the difference between "When you roll your eyes every time I try to talk about money, I feel really defeated and invisible" versus "You know,

Mr. High & Mighty, that friggin' eye roll thing you do is all the proof I need that you really are the asshole I always thought you were"? To be able to "fight" consciously and productively, you have to do your best to focus on behaviors or actions that aren't working for you and not go down the road of shaming and disrespecting who the other person really is. Remember, you're talking to your Beloved. It's fair game to criticize the behavior, but it's *no bueno* to criticize or try to tear down the other person. Would you put up with them doing that to you? (If you said "yes" to that question, you definitely want to do some deep work on what's up with your willingness to tolerate being trashed by *anyone*, much less your partner.)

- Compromising – There is something to be said for being able to let go of a position and also being willing to mutually agree to disagree. However, where possible, if you're fighting a battle that you really believe is worth fighting, then you've got to be ready to consider compromises when you can't be totally on the same page. Remember that notion that, if you can't agree on something, can you choose to *align* with one another's truths and choices freely and without ulterior motive or game playing ("I don't fully like it, but I will back your choice with the kids," for example)? If you can't get aligned with each other, then you want to look for compromises that solve a problem without either of you feeling like you just sold yourself and your integrity down the river. Don't have an unrealistic expectation that this process will be easy (though it *could* be, if you allow it to be).

- <u>Being respectful, no matter what</u> – The minute you get disparaging, vicious, cheap, nasty, physically intimidating, etc., you've lost the battle for sure, but you've also added fuel to losing the prime objective, which is having a relationship built to last with love, passion, and fulfillment. You won't get there if your partner feels unsafe and disrespected. Make no mistake that when you truly speak disrespectfully to your partner, particularly if you're doing it more often than not, what you're risking is a deterioration of trust that can be very difficult to come back from, no matter how often you apologized afterwards. So if you're tempted to go there, better to take your leave for a while, sort out what part of your inner family's been triggered, soothe that part, move your energy, and then come back. It's really not worth it to do it some other way.

5. Overcome Gridlock

When you both feel like you're gridlocked on something, it's essential to do the best you can to put on your compassion and empathy suit to try to understand your partner's underlying feelings that are getting in the way of coming to some kind of mutually acceptable resolution to the conflict. If you hold your relationship as the most precious of cargo, you need to develop the skill—through consistent practice—of being able to get your adult self in the driver's seat, with big pants on, to disengage from your distress enough to see where you can tap into your empathy with your partner. This alone creates room for you both to do the most key thing—maintain your heart connection with each other no matter what—that increases your likelihood of getting through just about anything. If you can't do that, you need to consider getting help because you're not very likely to be able to extricate yourselves from that disconnection on your own. While you may need to take breaks, compromise, and negotiate into the proverbial wee hours sometimes, trust and lean into your empathy and compassion with each other and don't give up until you have a resolution. If you really can't get there, then consider getting someone to help you break through it. One other tip: stay cognizant of the difference between bitching about something versus resolving something. You're bitching if you're bringing up problems with no intention or effort to get through it in any kind of good way. If you're serious about wanting to resolve something, then bring up the issue followed by saying something like, "What can we do to resolve this?" It's always better, in the long run, to get connected again than to be right.

6. Create Shared Meaning

It's certainly true that love has a fair amount of shared meaning for both people in a relationship, even if the *how* of that love may get expressed or shown differently. In spite of what Hollywood says, love won't always be enough to keep a built-to-last relationship lasting and thriving. One of the key things I've seen in my own marriage, particularly if I'm feeling pretty on it with Sarah about something, is how worthwhile and effective it is to reconnect with things that I *know* have shared meaning for us both. That can be memories of times we've shared that were really special and fun. It can also involve revisiting our values, attitudes, interests, and traditions. A key to longevity is to do that kind of revisiting both with open hearts and minds, without being attached to the value of the meaning staying stuck in the past. In other words, remembering past connections can reconnect you in the short term, but your long-term connection will thrive better if you're both open to discovering and co-creating new shared experiences and meanings with each other. Remember that values change over time, for example, as do attitudes. Consciously sharing with each other about that, discovering how your values are changing, and creating opportunities to exercise these evolving values and interests (both shared and different) will keep things organically evolving.

<u>Bonus Points</u>

I just want to add a few other things that should become habits for your individual happiness and your relationship's level of happiness.

- <u>Gratitude</u> – I can't possibly overstate the importance and benefit of cultivating and practicing what someone labeled "an attitude of gratitude." A lot of research has shown that grateful thinking promotes more appreciation and savoring of positive life experiences that, in turn, help "reprogram" your brain to focus more on the positive—which always feels better. Dr. Lyubomirsky's research has also shown that expressing gratitude beefs up your self-worth and self-esteem, and also helps you better cope with stress and trauma. Expressing and *feeling* gratitude (that's an important part, by the way ... you need to feel the gratitude, otherwise it may just be the shadow ego going through the motions without getting any real shift in your emotional state) are also likely to help you be more naturally inclined to be of caring service and support to others. This is good because it's pretty hard to stay in your own shit and negativity when you're loving on and serving someone else. It's also likely to make it harder to get stuck in comparisons that can take your mood down when you're truly appreciating what you have. Lastly, I dare you (if you can authentically and viscerally connect with gratitude about something or for someone) to be able to feel that gratitude and then simultaneously feel crappy.

- <u>Self-Compassion</u> – The shadow part of our ego hates this one. If you have compassion for yourself while your mind is mercilessly flogging you because you forgot your best friend's birthday, for example, then that shadow has nothing to do! It feels like it's out of a job. However, if you learn how to connect with those shadow parts of yourself and help them to basically redirect that energy toward what's right and good about you— even with your imperfections—those parts of the mind will eventually surrender to feeling good and helping you own your own worth, especially when you "screw up." While there are a lot of facets to this, I would say that a couple of the most important areas to practice this are (1) to remember that life does include suffering and adversity so that when it's your turn to go through that in some way, you don't personalize it and become a victim, but embrace it compassionately as an opportunity; and (2) to remember that being human means that you're mortal, vulnerable, and imperfect (as much as you may want to believe you're a special exception), so there's no point beating yourself up inside because you irrationally believe you're the only one suffering.

- <u>Forgiveness</u> – No relationship will be a built-to-last one without the presence of strong forgiveness muscles. When you and your partner are really struggling with each other, or finding yourselves dead in the water in terms of being able to reconnect with each other, it's a sure sign that something hasn't been forgiven, either with the other, yourself, or both. There are numerous definitions of forgiveness, but here are two that I really like: (1) giving of yourself the way you did before you took yourself away; and (2) resolving your objections to your own life by making peace with the times you didn't get what you wanted and objected to it. In my experience, forgiveness really is a state of being, especially internally.

  Recently, after decades of struggle and working on my issues with my mom, I had a breakthrough of forgiving her for all of it, which came as a result of realizing that I was fed up with my life being hijacked by my own unwillingness to let go of my pain and rage with her ... combined with connecting to my huge ability to empathize with just about anyone. When I was willing to do that, it was a full-body experience of release and a huge inner space opening up energetically. None of that would've happened had I not made a *decision* to forgive, no matter what it took.

  When you and your partner are really jammed up with each other, isolating, and disconnecting, the odds are pretty slim that you're going to be able to reconcile and reconnect with the Belovedness of each other without first forgiving. This will become easier if you've got a standing commitment to yourself, your partner, and your relationship to do whatever it takes to help you feel better about a situation. This can include trying on different perspectives regarding what happened; giving up expecting things from other people or your life that they don't choose to give you; looking at what rules you've set up internally for yourself and others that are unenforceable and unreasonable; and looking for what archaic and inaccurate story you have about yourself (that you're ready to let go of) that *not* forgiving allows you to hang on to until you fully poison yourself.

- <u>Laughter</u> – When was the last time you can remember laughing so hard you thought you were going to pee yourself all the while focusing on how pissed off you were at someone? If you're like all other human beings, you'd be hard-pressed to come up with such a memory because you *can't* focus on something "bad" and laugh at the same time. When you're feeling down in the dumps, in general, or you find yourself running into your cave to isolate and mope, practice making the choice to connect to whatever you find funny— and then laugh! Whether it's listening to a comedy routine, watching *Funny or Die* videos, reading a joke book you love, or watching something that just makes you feel good *and* laugh, you *always* have a choice regarding how you're feeling, even if your mind is screaming that you don't. You'll build more faith in that the more you practice taking charge of your state, own that you're the only one at true cause for your state, and start getting cracked up. Laughing relieves tension and relaxes your muscles throughout your body for about forty-five minutes according to some studies. It also helps boost your immune system, releases all those happy-feeling endorphins, and improves your blood-vessel functioning and blood flow, which helps protect you from heart attacks. Need I say more about why this is one of the cheapest and fastest ways to get yourself back on track with your best and brightest self?

Keeping all of these pieces in mind (and heart) and practicing them consistently will go a tremendous way toward helping you both take responsibility for your emotional states, the state of your relationship, and your power and ability to be able to effect the changes and growth you both want in your relationship.

Remember, simply compiling more information won't transform what isn't working in your relationship. It can *help*, to be sure. But just like you could buy 100 maps, if you never take a trip, what the hell's the point? So I encourage you to take hold of the fact that living life in constant reaction; not taking ownership of your power (and how to use it to get what you want in the best possible way) to create your own experience of life and love; and not practicing as if you're life depended on it are one-way tickets to suffering. As my dear friend and mentor, Shakti Dudley, first told me in 1993 as she was showing me how to get my head out of my ass, "Suffering is optional!" May it be so for you and your Beloved as you walk down this conscious pathway to your relationship that will be built-to-last.

Section IV

From Happily Ever After to Bliss

———————————•●•———————————

Well, here we are in the home stretch of the book. So far, you've learned all kinds of things and gotten my perspectives on how you can design, build, and maintain a passionate, lasting, and loving relationship. One of my strongest opinions on what it takes to pull this off is to stay awake to the fact that there's no "happily ever after" to reach, at least in the way Hollywood and the media still like to dangle the carrot out in front of us to this day. None of what's been shared with you in this book is meant to feed that mythology.

What I've tried to do is to offer real-life experiences (using real-life language), techniques/tools, and wisdom that isn't really unique, but *is* meant to be usable and to shake up the ways you're used to thinking about—and doing—relationship. I've stated throughout the book that the primary reason for being in relationship (besides the fact that we're hard-wired to be in relationship and related) is to fast track our personal and spiritual growth and evolution. If you resonate with that point of view, which I have to imagine you do if you've gotten *this* far in the book, then I encourage you not to settle for anything less than vibrant, conscious relationship. Don't just be ok with some version of happily ever after. Webster's defines "bliss" as "complete happiness." What I've found in my marriage and life, as well as with all the clients I've coached over the years, is that a minimum requirement for being happy is to attain mastery of your internal (*not* external) states and being at peace with who you are and with what is, in any given moment.

The Four Noble Truths of Buddhism point out that our biggest source of suffering comes, essentially, from resisting what is. It isn't that you can't or shouldn't shift things that don't work for you, yet so much of what we try to do is to bend life to our will and eliminate what doesn't feel good or hurts. A more viable and blissful alternative is to start from a place of accepting what is as an ever-present growth opportunity and go from there to capitalizing on what's up *now* to guide you toward what you're really longing for (instead of avoiding something). This will provide much more consistent motivation for staying dedicated to continually growing yourself and your relationship.

This may mean, by the way, that—in spite of your best efforts (or non-effort) to co-create a relationship built to last with your sweetie—that your path to bliss requires you to leave your relationship. So, before I leave you with some of the key bullet points to remember to grow your bliss, let's look at some of the signs that indicate you may need to end a relationship as part of being aligned with what your Spirit knows is your true path.

When It's Time to Seriously Consider Ending the Relationship

Some would say that you shouldn't be in a relationship if you don't love each other anymore. On the face of that, that would seem logical and wise. However, one thing I've seen over and over again is that feeling out of love isn't always accurate or real. It may just mean that you've both allowed so much debris and shit to get piled on top of that love that you simply can't access it. That's very different from it being dead and *gone*.

Before you say you're complete with each other, you need to ask yourself if there's even a burning *ember* of love still there, at least. I've worked with relationships that looked hopelessly broken and irreparable, but there were still *some* embers of genuine love and caring there from which to be able to reinvent and reinvigorate a whole *new* relationship. (Think about it: would you be so hurt and pissed off if you really didn't care about and miss what you *know* is possible?) If there truly isn't even an ember, it's damn near impossible to resurrect a dead fire. In cases like that, it becomes about seeing how you can consciously design and build a sacred, compassionate, and respectful transition out of the relationship and, if you have kids at home, to building a co-parenting relationship that honors the best of everyone without allowing anger and grief to pollute what your children are going to have to process and integrate in the best way possible.

If there are embers or more available, then I'm a big fan of doing the best you can possibly do (with outside help, because you wouldn't be in this kind of state if you knew how to do it differently yourselves) to give the unworkable relationship a proper funeral and then see what you can build newly with each other. It makes no rational or loving sense to let go of something you've invested so much time, energy, and experiences in without giving it everything you've got to turn it around. To do that with a strong chance for success, you have to have *some* love accessible, you still have to care, and you have to be willing to get brutally honest with yourself about your role in the deterioration that's happened. You can't build anew if you insist on blaming each other for *your* unhappiness. You have to be willing to take full responsibility for your experience and your 50 percent ownership of the success or failure of the relationship. If you don't have those things in place, it's time to get out, because I haven't seen anyone turn things around without those elements in place.

It's also time to leave a relationship when it's gotten pervasively toxic to one or both of you. When either of you and/or the relationship has gotten toxic, no one wins, no matter how hard you try to pretend that's not true. It isn't that toxicity is an automatic "I'm out of here"—I want to make that really clear. The presence of toxicity means that you've hit a place where ignoring it will almost surely mean the eventual and likely end of the relationship; it just becomes a matter of how much everyone involved is going to suffer needlessly. Put another way: if things have gotten *truly* toxic, it's the last sign that you either (1) get help and do your best to turn it around (letting it rise or fall on the quality of the work you do to turn things around), or (2) it's time to get out for your own well-being.

Here are some signs you're now in that toxic state:

- One or both of you are continually abusive to each other, be it emotionally, physically, mentally, or sexually; you've sought help with no success; and/or it's happening with the children too. Again, I emphasize that this is a criteria for leaving *if* you've *both* gotten help, done what your therapist or coach has told you to do, and found that it just isn't changing.

- You're trying to carry it and change it all on your own. I quoted the statistic that 80 percent of the time, women are the ones who initiate change and healing in a relationship. In twenty years of practice, I've had two men (yes, I said two) initiate an inquiry into getting help. I know there are tons of men out there who are miserable and want to get it all better, but they don't act on it until their partner says, "We work on it or else." That's all by way of making the point that a relationship cannot be repaired or reinvented without both parties being committed, involved, and invested in the same desired outcome. While I'm loathe to be absolute about much, this is one thing I err on the side of being absolute about: if your partner refuses to get help and do his or her work, it's time to get out.

- You're staying in the relationship fundamentally to fulfill a need to rescue or save someone, otherwise known as "social worker syndrome." If your main source of feeling valued and worthwhile is to cast your needs aside and save someone from ruin, the relationship's toxic from the get-go.

- One or both of you are incapable (*unwilling* is actually *more* the truth) of being mature (meaning you're committed to and doing your best to practice the six paths to a happy relationship that are laid out in Chapter 15). When you've become unable to be respectful, vulnerable, empathetic, compassionate (with self and the other), and willing to own your part, things are on the path to being fatally toxic to the relationship if not already so.

- You consistently don't feel physically and/or emotionally safe with your partner, especially while getting professional help ... or after. If you're not safe, you can't trust, and without trust, your relationship can't work.

- Your health is deteriorating.

- You're turning to substances just to cope with how unhappy you are.

- Your children are exhibiting signs of physical, emotional, and/or psychological trauma. You want to remember that children feel *everything,* even if nothing's being said out loud. They become shock absorbers for the relationship, which should not be their job. If you start noticing fundamentally different behaviors cropping up—particularly signs of withdrawal and contraction when they've usually been outgoing and social—you have reason to be concerned that they're taking on the brunt of your relationship's toxicity.

- You've hired at least three or four different therapists/coaches, and nothing's worked. If you're in *that* boat (unless you both just have horrible tastes in picking your helpers), I think that's a sign that you just don't care anymore, but you don't have the courage to admit it and move on ... and *that's* toxic.

Now, there are probably many more, but this list is a good enough starting point to assess where you are on the toxicity scale and decide what you're going to do about it. If you're not willing to do anything, I strongly suggest *that's* a time to end it as well. My final absolute criteria for ending a relationship (based on my professional experience and shares from many colleagues in the therapeutic community) is if you're with someone who's truly a narcissist. I'm not talking about someone who's just self-absorbed, because we *all* are to one extent or another. That can be changed, and it would be when a self-absorbed person is also self-aware enough to realize they've gotten unhealthily self-absorbed. But if you're with someone who fits most of the diagnostic criteria for narcissistic personality disorder, they aren't even capable of being self-aware (subjectively or objectively) in a transparent, honest way with themselves or others. There's a useful, nonclinical, but pretty accurate article on how to recognize you may be living with a narcissist at http://www.halcyon.com/jmashmun/npd/howto.html.

I'd encourage you to read that. It isn't rigorously scientific, but it's pretty on target ... close enough for government work. If you're in a relationship with someone like that and have children with them, I'd also strongly suggest (based on seventeen years of leading inner child healing workshops) that you will be doing your children no long- or short-term favors staying with someone like that. That kind of parent isn't really capable of being a healthy parent to a child, and the child will spend most of their time—like living with an addict—having their energy and trust sucked out of them, because such people end up becoming the central focus of a family unit, literally making it all about *them*. Our children deserve better than that.

You may be wondering by now what this buzz kill-ish material has to do with bliss! It's actually simple if you buy my notion that bliss comes from being your most authentic, Spirit-led self, with no apologies and no exceptions, and loving all of it (or at least being compassionate and forgiving of the less pretty or nice parts). So, what you refuse to see with brutal honesty, self-compassion, and transparency (which would mean that shame is running your life's show to a large degree) will keep you engineering and managing your life oriented toward hiding what you judge to be bad and missing all that's good. You'll also make decisions (unconsciously most of the time,) based on what you *don't* want seen and/or just simply don't like. In *this* framework of bliss, relationship isn't what actually *causes* bliss, but it becomes a great proverbial sandbox in which to discover, play with, and expand upon your bliss, while giving your partner (and children, if you have them) the opportunity to do the same.

Wrapping It Up

So, if you're willing to take on designing, building, and maintaining a relationship (and a life) built to last – which will give you *so* many rich chances to learn, embody, and practice your unique version of bliss - then here are the non-negotiable (to me) elements for achieving such a blissful way of being (across the board) that you want to do your best to keep front and center:

- Remember it isn't always about you, but it always *starts* with you. Be as clear as you can be (and get help getting clear when you need it) about who you are, what you value most, what you like, what you despise, what you long for, and why you feel you're even here. Then, share that with your friends, your lover/partner, your family (where it feels safe to do so), and orient your choices, as much as possible, toward what brings you joy, fun, and a strong connection to what's good that you have and want to add to the party. And, be sure that you stay congruent with that, while never forgetting that no one but you is responsible for your experience of your life moment-to-moment.

- Never stop learning and growing. Remember that Dylan song: One who isn't busy growing is busy dying. This is a key principle in life and in relationships of all kinds. A corollary to this would be to never settle, either. It never works, if your aim is to have true bliss. In your relationship, keep looking for opportunities to stretch yourself and support your partner in doing the same, separately and as a couple.

- Make having fun a very high priority in your relationship to life and with your partner. Life is literally too short to waste it waiting for some magical state to arrive (like retirement) before you can let yourself let it all hang out and have a blast as much as possible. With your love partner, nothing can help break a dry or tight spell like having a laughing fit together.

- Never take anything—especially your partner—for granted. It's disrespectful and robs you of what you can each learn by always remaining curious about who you both are now, rather than staying attached to a version of each other that's in the past. I'm always learning more about Sarah after all these years, and that's fun. A good way to avoid this is to regularly check in with each other—not about mundane logistics, but about how each of you are feeling about life, your work, your bodies, your dreams and desires, and each other. Stay current with each other as a *standing commitment*, in other words.

- Live as a committed being. Without commitment, you're just like a jellyfish blobbing your way through life being batted around by the whims of the sea. Know what you're committed to, surround yourselves with people who will help you stay accountable to those commitments, and celebrate all your wins with each other.

- Focus more on what you have that's good, not on what you think you're missing. I don't want you or your desires to ever stop evolving, but too many people in relationships stay locked on—with the five-finger death grip—to what they don't have or are worried they'll lose, before even letting themselves enjoy and savor what's already here that's pretty damn great. That's a much more empowering launch pad for growth and a life of great positivity.

- Keep looking for the edges of your comfort zones and go past them—to whatever degree—to keep you and your relationship from stagnating.

- When in doubt, communicate. Retire your eggshell walkin' shoes!

I'm sure I've missed some, but you surely won't go wrong with any of these. Each one of us deserves to fully be who we authentically are and to find the bliss and freedom that comes from feeling and being self-love and self-acceptance (the good, the bad, and the ugly) ... and being that way with all you touch. Your heart—even when hurt or broken—will always be your most powerful touchstone if you'll just listen to it, allow yourself to trust it, let yourself feel it fully, and give it at every available opportunity. That, right there, will give you a built-to-last *life* that's passionate, ever engaging, stimulating in the best ways, and—to quote one of my clients—a life you don't want to take a vacation from.

.

Acknowledgements

As I imagine it to be for most first-time authors, I never could've imagined what the process was actually going to involve or be like to experience. What started out as resistance to writing a book for about 30 years became a soul- and heart-enriching process that I wouldn't have been able to do without the support, love, cheerleading, ass-kicking (in many cases), wisdom, and inspiration of some very precious and key people in my life.

First, to all of my past and present clients, I can't thank you enough for entrusting me with your most vulnerable, intimate, and oft-scary parts of yourselves and your relationships. You all have taught me so much more than you probably could even imagine. This book would literally never have happened

To my brothers in my Evolved Man community that have graciously empowered me to lead them towards their greatness as men and return the favor in kind, thank you for your love, support, brotherhood, and courage.

To the men I sat in circle with for so many years within the Mankind Project Community in Durango, and the Cornerstones Brothers in the Bay Area who will ALWAYS have a treasured and beloved place in my heart for all you showed me and brought out of me as a leader and mentor of men.

To my publisher and mentor, Robbin Simons, thank you for hearing the message that was waiting to be shared, reaching out to ask if you could publish this book, and hand-holding me through it with seemingly inhuman patience and grace.

To the specific clients that have cheered me on (and you know who you are) to do this book, thank you for belief in me and your appreciation of what I had to say that you *insisted* others MUST be able to get.

Lastly, a HUGE "Thank you" to my team that have helped me keep my business running more smoothly than it should've while I've been immersed in writing this: Colleen Davis, Terri Williams, Walter Brown, Sandra Winter, and eVision Media (Daniel Simmons & Susan Friesen). You have no idea how much I appreciate you, your work, and your belief in what I'm up to.

About the Author,

Geoff Laughton

Geoff Laughton is an outspoken and lively Master Coach, Presentational Speaker, Transformational Author, NLP Practitioner, and Seminar Facilitator with over 20 years expertise counseling and coaching throughout the US. Geoff passionately gets powerful results for clients in many life challenges – but, in particular, with the pain of being in a relationship that isn't working.

Geoff was propelled into this 20-years and counting track he is on as a result of his utter disillusionment and exhaustion from spending 15 years in the corporate world, which left him feeling like he was a card-carrying member of the walking dead. Exhausted, 100 pounds overweight, and burnt out - that mediocre and soul-sucking professional life fueled him to commit strongly to his own growth without compromise.

He eagerly propelled himself into many realms of personal development towards that end, passionately studying and learning as a workshop participant in *many* different modalities. In doing so, he made the huge discovery that he had forgotten his gifts and longing to help others find a life free of mediocrity and settling. This re-connection inspired him to spend years training to lead workshops and coach as a powerful example of conscious masculinity doing his best to live with a fully open heart connected to Source.

In particular, Geoff spent two years being trained by Inner World Seminars to lead his own Intensives targeted at getting underneath chronic issues plaguing clients that were based in our development years of 0-7 or 7-14, where we form most of our belief systems. Geoff is one of only 3 people in the world certified to lead that body of work. That intimate weekend broke over a thousand people through to a new way of relating to the inner Parts of themselves that had previously kept them separated from the Goals and relationships they were looking to attain.

Continuing his relentless journey of self-renaissance, he spent several years expanding his toolkit through participating in and leading hundreds of transformational workshops, retreats, and intensives, along with spending over 15 years training with Spiritual Masters and top-drawer Change Agents/Coaches.

One of the most impactful trainings was the powerful Mankind Project's New Warrior Training Adventure. It clued him into the heart of what is missing for men in our world today, which is really a huge void for a great many men. That experience, and all he learned, led Geoff to evolve into becoming a leader amongst men. Since 2000, Geoff has led over 50 men's retreats with the organization he co-founded (The Cornerstones Foundation), and has facilitated over 500 men's group meetings. He continues to facilitate twice monthly men's groups that include both men in Geoff's home area of Boulder, Colorado and men from around the U.S. who participate virtually.

An eloquent conversationalist and highly intuitive Coach, Geoff is able to navigate through even the most challenging topics clients bring in with ease. Over a thousand clients all over the world have a better life now because of his vast training and experience. He has created a body of work designed to help people in relationship trouble, couples, singles and men who found themselves wanting, like he did, to reach for something greater.

With his consistent reaching for higher realms of what is possible in living one's heart boldly and without compromise, Geoff has made learning to love full out the legacy he would like to leave to the world.

About Geoff's Work

Geoff has never lost track of how it felt, in the midst of a 16-year corporate career, to be walking around as a card-carrying member of the Walking Dead. It's been his non-negotiable commitment over the last 20 years to never live like that again – *and to do what he can to be sure no one else does either* – that has helped him build a very successful second career as a Relationship Architect, Transformational Author, Men's Work Leader, Motivational Speaker, and Retreat Facilitator.

Geoff teaches individuals and couples how to design, build, and maintain the relationship with themselves and each other that expands connection, healing, and creates harmony with their Spirits' dreams that have been neglected and/or forgotten.

To-date, Geoff has worked with hundreds of private clients and couples; has led hundreds of workshops; facilitated numerous life-altering retreats around the country for men, women, and couples; and has spoken at many live and online transformational events.

Connect with Geoff Laughton

Websites: www.yourrelationshiparchitect.com & http://www.builttolastbook.com/

Facebook: www.facebook.com/RecoveringYourRelationshipGeoffLaughton

LinkedIn: www.linkedin.com/in/geofflaughton

Twitter: www.twitter.com/geofflaughton

Blog: www.yourrelationshiparchitect.com/blog

In Gratitude to You...

Thank you for listening to your heart and gut in purchasing **Built To Last**. I know it's a significant investment of time you're making for your growth and happiness.

Because this book is also an expression of *my* passionate commitment to healthier relationships and families on the planet, the more people that read it, the more impact that can be made.

If you're willing to help that happen, I would be so grateful if you could take a minute or two to share what you loved about this book and provide an honest review on our Amazon sales page.

Resources

Brickman & Campbell (1971): Hedonic Relativism and planning the good society. New York: Academic Press. Pp. 287-302

Brene Brown, Ph.D. (2010): The Gifts of Imperfection: Let Go of Who You Think You're Supposed to Be and Embrace Who You Are. Center City, MN; Hazelden Press

Daniel Goleman, Ph.D. (1998): Working with Emotional Intelligence, NY: Bantam Books

Michael Eysenck, Ph.D.: research on Hedonic Treadmill retrieved from Wikipedia.org

Rick Hanson, Ph.D. (2013): Hardwiring Happiness. New York, NY: Harmony Publishing

Augustine Kposowa, Ph.D.; Journal of Epidemiology & Community Health. 01/2004; :p. 993. Source: PubMed

Sonya Lyubomirsky, Ph.D. (2007): The How of Happiness: A New Approach To Getting The Life You Want; Penguin Group

Martin E. Seligman, Ph.D. (2011): Learned Optimism: How to Change Your Mind and Your Life (Vintage); Knopf Doubleday Publishing Group

Nan Silver, Ph.D. & John Gottman, Ph.D. (1999). The Seven Principles for Making a Marriage Work. New York, NY: Three Rivers Press

Made in the USA
Middletown, DE
21 August 2015